124749

The Reform of Direct Taxation

Report of the Fabian Taxation Review Committee

The Reform of Direct Taxation

Report of the Direct Taxation Review Committee

The Reform of Direct Taxation

Report of the Fabian Taxation Review Committee

Fabian Society

Published by the Fabian Society
11 Dartmouth Street
London SW1H 9BN
United Kingdom

ISBN 0 7163 3505 0

Cover design: Brian Nugent

Printed by
The College Hill Press Limited (TU)
London & Worthing

TNS : QAR R
1990

Contents

Chairman's Preface

The idea for the establishment of this Committee came from a meeting organised by the Fabian Society after the 1987 General Election. I should like to thank John Willman, General Secretary, and the Fabian Society as a whole, for having followed up this initiative and found the finance necessary to set up the Committee and support its activities. Particular thanks are due to the Webb Trust. We are also indebted to British Petroleum, who arranged a valuable meeting with their Tax Group, and who prepared papers for the Committee.

The resources available to the Committee made it possible to appoint Holly Sutherland of LSE as the Secretary/Researcher to the Committee. Her contribution has been quite invaluable. She has organised the Committee's meetings, prepared papers for these meetings, carried out research for the Committee, authored or co-authored several of the Background Papers, and liaised with the Fabian Society and other bodies. The preparation of this report, to a tight schedule, has been a particular achievement, in which she has been assisted by John Willman, whose software skills have been most helpful, by Sue Coles, who provided secretarial help, and by Karen Gardiner and Ann Harding who contributed research assistance at crucial stages.

In the course of the Committee's work we have been considerably assisted by papers prepared for us by Michael Devereux, Henry Neuburger and Stephen Smith. We have received helpful comments on our work from Fran Bennett, Andrew Coulson, Peter Esam, Mark Robson, Nicholas Stern and Alister Sutherland. We are most grateful to all of these people, but should emphasise that they have no responsibility for the views expressed in this Report.

Finally, I would like to thank the members of the Committee, who gave up a considerable amount of valuable time to the work of the Committee, and Emma Maclennan who participated as an observer until she went on maternity leave in March 1989. They all contributed to making it an enjoyable and stimulating experience.

Tony Atkinson

Members of the Taxation Review Committee

The Review Committee was chaired by **TONY ATKINSON FBA**, Professor of Economics at the London School of Economics, President of the European Economic Association and former member of the Royal Commission on the Distribution of Income & Wealth. The membership of the Committee covered a range of areas of experience and expertise:

TONY CHRISTOPHER CBE – Chairman of the Trades Union Congress and formerly General Secretary of the Inland Revenue Staff Federation. A former member of the Royal Commission on the Distribution of Income & Wealth.

LORD GREGSON DL – Director of Fairey Group plc, Director of British Steel Plc, member of the House of Lords Select Committee on Science & Technology, President of the Defence Manufacturers Association and immediate Past President of The Parliamentary & Scientific Committee.

JOHN HILLS – Senior Research Fellow in the Suntory-Toyota International Centre for Economics & Related Disciplines at the London School of Economics, former research officer at the Institute for Fiscal Studies and on the staff of the House of Commons Treasury & Civil Service Select Committee.

OONAGH MCDONALD – formerly Member of Parliament for Thurrock and Labour Treasury Spokeswoman, now Visiting Fellow at Warwick University.

BILL MCKENZIE – chartered accountant, formerly a partner with Price Waterhouse, now a taxation consultant.

Chapter 1

Introduction and summary

Aim of the Review

The Fabian Society Taxation Review was launched in Spring 1988 to carry out a critical examination of the British tax system and to draw up proposals for reform which could be the basis for Labour's policy in the 1990s.

There is a strong case for an overall investigation of the British tax system, there having been no major inquiry since the Meade Committee in the 1970s. In particular, there is a need to assemble an integrated set of proposals based on analysis of the shortcomings of the present taxes. This analysis in itself will, we hope, perform a valuable informative function. Knowledge about the tax system among the population as a whole is very limited. Although the Government has managed to divert attention away from the rise in the overall tax burden and highlighted the fall in the basic rate of income tax, many people polled after the 1987 election did not know the level of the basic rate. It is not therefore surprising that tax policy is surrounded by myths — both about what has happened and what are the alternatives. It is hoped that the Fabian Review will contribute to public debate about policy in the field of taxation, dispelling the myths and demonstrating that there are alternatives, which are both feasible and attractive, to the present Conservative policies.

The remit of the Review is the British tax system. At the same time, it has taken account of the overlap between taxation and social security, and issues such as the poverty trap have been the subject of consideration. While our concern has been with the development of British tax policy, we have taken account of the experience of tax reform in other countries, and the implications of the European Community and the common internal market.

Work of the Review Committee

The Committee has held a series of meetings since it was set up in January 1988 and has considered papers on a variety of subjects. It has also received submissions from a number of individuals and organisations, and we would like to thank those who have contributed to its work in this way. We have been able to draw extensively on *Changing Tax*, by one of our members (John Hills), published by the Child Poverty Action Group Ltd. in January 1989, and on research carried out by the Committee's Secretary (Holly Sutherland) on the effect of both current Government policy and proposed reforms.

During this period, the Committee has published several Background Papers which are listed at the end of the Report. These Background Papers are published as a contribution to the public debate about taxation but do not necessarily represent the views of the Committee.

The Report does not cover the whole range of taxes. As its title indicates, the Report concentrates on *direct* taxation. The Committee has published a Background Paper (number 5) on indirect taxation by Henry Neuburger, but its schedule of completing work on the Report by the end of 1989 did not allow it time to examine the issues in sufficient depth to cover the subject here.

Objective of the Report

Our Report covers income tax, company taxation, National Insurance contributions, local taxation and capital taxation. These are major topics, on which much public attention is focussed. In our view they are subjects on which Labour can offer a distinct and attractive alternative. Fairer and more effective direct taxation is quite within our reach and it is important that this message should be put across effectively.

This Report seeks to spell out the arguments which should lie behind Labour's approach and suggest ways in which the principles may be translated into action. We do not imagine that the policy proposals described here will be accepted in full by a future Labour Chancellor, but they demonstrate that Labour's aims are realistically achievable.

In this Report, we are taking no view about the level of public spending. The structure that we describe is one that is consistent either with raising the same amount of tax revenue as at present, or with financing further spending, or with the possibility that overall tax burdens may actually be lower. Just as Mrs Thatcher has raised the share of taxes in national income, so it may fall under Mr Kinnock.

Summary of principal conclusions of this Report

The primary objective of the tax system (Chapter 2) should be to raise revenue for vital public services in a way that is fair and which attracts public confidence. Fairness means that each of us should be treated in an even-handed way and that those on low incomes should pay a smaller proportion of their income in tax than those who are higher paid. In addition, taxation should be designed as far as possible, to promote Britain's economic performance, rather than undermine it; and we should seek to reduce the ways in which taxation may distort business decisions and choices people make about their lives. Labour's plans for taxation should be forward-looking to the 1990s, taking account of changing economic and social circumstances and of Britain's international responsibilities, including a wider role in the European Community.

The Conservative Government has both increased taxation and unfairly redistributed its burden (Chapter 3). VAT and National Insurance contributions have increased at the same time as income tax has been reduced. The overall effect is that those on average earnings pay nearly as large a fraction of their income in tax as those earning half as much again. The aim of Labour's policy is to increase the degree of progression and in this respect the personal direct taxes covered in this Report have a large role to play.

The base for the personal direct tax system (Chapter 4) should in our view be a comprehensive income tax, including all additions to a person's resources, subject to departures from this base justified by reasons of principle or practical necessity. The Committee is not persuaded that all savings should be exempt, as under an expenditure tax, but recognises that there are grounds for providing privileged treatment for particular forms of savings (such as pension contributions). In our detailed analysis of the tax base (Chapter 7), we aim to balance the case for privileged treatment against the benefits from broadening the tax base and hence allowing tax rates to be lowered.

The key elements to our proposed reform of personal direct taxation are:

● **Graduation**: the rate structure for the personal income tax (Chapter 5) should be graduated, with a zero rate band followed by rates rising from below the existing basic rate to a maximum of 50 per cent. The structure of employee National Insurance contributions should be made fully progressive (Chapter 8) with contributions paid only on earnings above the threshold and the upper earnings limit abolished. A graduated structure would allow the same tax revenue to be raised as at present while at the same time cutting the tax paid by the majority, reversing the unfair redistribution of the tax burden under the Conservatives.

● **Independence**: the basic principle of taxation for husbands and wives (Chapter 6) should be that of independence, with fully separate taxation and full privacy in tax affairs. The Committee recommends that there should be a substantial increase in the single person's allowance, while holding constant the total of the single person's and the married couple's allowance, and that a continuation of this policy at successive budgets would allow the married couple's allowance to be phased out. The additional personal allowance for single parents should similarly be phased out.

● **Broadening the income tax base**: the income tax base should be broadened (Chapter 7), to allow a given revenue to be raised with lower rates, and to treat more fairly different kinds of income. This base broadening would continue the erosion of mortgage interest relief, as has taken place under the Conservatives. It would limit all lump-sum payments under occupational pensions, and would eliminate a whole series of tax exemptions (private medical insurance, Business Expansion Schemes, Personal Equity Plans, share options and profit sharing schemes). Fringe benefits should be added to the base for National Insurance contributions (Chapter 8). A charge on investment income in excess of a threshold should be levied as a social security tax (Chapter 8), and the same charge should be applied to capital gains (Chapter 9), and to the income and capital gains of pension funds.

Our Report makes proposals in three further important areas of taxation.

● **Capital taxation**: the Committee recommends for immediate action that the Inheritance Tax be abolished and replaced by either a toughened Capital Transfer Tax or a new Lifetime Capital Receipts Tax (Chapter 9). Alternatively, wealth transfers should be brought within the income tax base. It also recommends major changes to capital gains taxation.

● **Business and corporate taxation**: the Committee recommends (Chapter 10) that in broad terms the existing structure of corporation tax be retained, with regard to both the definition of taxable profits and the rate structure, retaining a system of imputation. In the case of the self-employed, we recommend a change to a current year basis of assessment and a review of the definition of tax-deductible expenses. A change in the structure of employer National Insurance contributions is proposed (Chapter 8), introducing a fully graduated schedule and extending the tax base to include fringe benefits.

● **Local taxation**: the Committee concluded that there are substantial difficulties in providing an immediate replacement for the poll tax and that there are considerable doubts about the feasibility of a local income tax (Chapter 11). The Committee's preference is that the eventual replacement should take the form of a capital value rate, which might be accompanied by a regional income tax, and recommends that these be more fully investigated by an incoming Labour government. Immediate action is necessary to remove the worst features of the poll tax, but the extent to which transitional measures are introduced depends on the situation at the time and the amount of revenue which is to be raised by local taxes on households.

In framing our recommendations, we have been careful to pay attention to the constraints which the practicalities of administration place on reform. In Chapter 12 we consider the administrative procedures necessary, particularly to allow for a graduated rate structure. We conclude that the proposals made in the Report are indeed administratively feasible, particularly when account is taken of the fact that they will be phased in over a period of time. The introduction of graduation will involve some increase in the workload of the Inland Revenue, but there will also be some simplifications of the tax system which will liberate administrative resources. The efficient organisation of the Revenue, and the provision of a proper level of staffing, will no doubt be priorities for a Labour government. It is essential that there be public confidence that taxation is being collected in an equitable and effective manner. We make a number of recommendations for more effective measures to limit avoidance and evasion.

The above summary is intended to convey the essence of our findings; a full list of recommendations is set out in the Conclusions at the end of the Report.

Chapter 2

Objectives of taxation

The aim of this chapter is to provide a brief statement of the objectives of taxation and to relate tax reform to wider economic and social changes. It goes almost without saying that we do not attempt to provide either an extensive philosophical discussion of principles of justice or a detailed account of social change in Britain. The purpose is to set the scene for the subsequent analysis and the emphasis is on practical implications.

Objectives of taxation: financing public services

Our starting point is that revenues have to be raised to finance vital public services. This is non-controversial in that all political parties accept the need for public spending. Even those who would like to minimise the role of government still acknowledge that the state has to ensure law and order.

What is controversial is the size of the revenue requirement. Here Labour has all too often been forced on to the defensive. In our view, Labour should start from the positive statement that public spending has a major role to play in *enabling* people to live their lives and carry on their economic activities. There are certain things which are the essentials of a modern civilised society. As other countries have recognised, public spending has a positive function in building pathways out of poverty, in providing key infrastructure for business, and in providing facilities which we can enjoy in common. Transfers, in the form of social security and other benefits, are essential to protect people from ill-fortune and to provide for the needs of the family life-cycle. While most people have ambivalent feelings towards paying their own taxes, and some may resent the fact that others appear to be paying less, we believe that there is widespread acceptance of the need to contribute to financing of public spending.

Under a Labour Government, public spending would no doubt take different forms. The Party has indicated that areas like education and training, health, the environment, science and technology would receive higher priority. Other areas would be cut or made more efficient. We do not attempt to take a view here as to whether the overall level of spending would be higher or lower than at present. The level of spending, and the tax revenue required to support it will of course depend on the particular macro-economic situation inherited from the preceding government.

Objectives of taxation: a fair distribution of the tax burden

The First Report of Labour's Policy Review described a "fair tax system" as

"one that treats each of us in an even-handed way, and achieves a fair distribution of income and wealth throughout the community" (page 21).

The first of these attributes we take to mean that people in broadly similar circumstances should pay broadly similar amounts of tax. This principle of "equal treatment of equals" is often referred to as *horizontal equity*. We believe that this is an important principle, not only in its own right but also because of its effect on public perceptions of the tax system. The tax system will be regarded as capricious if £10,000 of income from one source is taxed while £10,000 from another, apparently equivalent, source goes tax-free.

Considerations of horizontal equity will play a particularly significant role when we come to the issue of the tax base discussed in principle in Chapter 4 and in detail in Chapter 7. It is, of course, always open to debate what one means by people being in "similar circumstances", and in our proposals we have allowed for some differences in view. It may also be the case that it is necessary to over-ride horizontal equity considerations in order to achieve other objectives, such as the encouragement of particular forms of activity. At the same time, we feel that under the present tax system there are a number of provisions which are manifestly inequitable in a horizontal sense, and which have no other over-riding justification.

The second attribute of a fair tax system described by the Policy Review is concerned with the relative burden on people with different levels of income. This is typically called *vertical equity* to distinguish it from horizontal equity. Here it is a basic principle of Britain's income tax — and of income tax systems throughout the world — that the proportion of income paid in tax is a larger proportion at higher income levels. A person with an income of £30,000 should pay a larger proportion of this income than a person, otherwise equally placed, with an income of £15,000. A tax such that the proportion collected rises with income is referred to as a *progressive* tax.

Whether or not a tax is progressive may be seen from the *average rate of tax,* or the proportion of income paid in tax. For example, in 1989 a single person with earnings of £15,000 paid £3,054 income tax, which represented 20.4 per cent of earnings. A single person with earnings of double that amount paid £7,781 income tax, or 25.9 per cent, so that the proportion collected rises with income. (No account is taken here of mortgage interest relief or other deductions; nor do the calculations include National Insurance contributions.) The progression of the 1989/90 income tax system for a single person with no extra reliefs is shown in Chart 2.1. The average tax rate starts from zero at the level of the personal allowance (£2,785) and reaches 25.9 per cent at the highest level of income shown on the Chart (£30,000 a year).

Chart 2.1: Income tax structure 1989/90
Single person

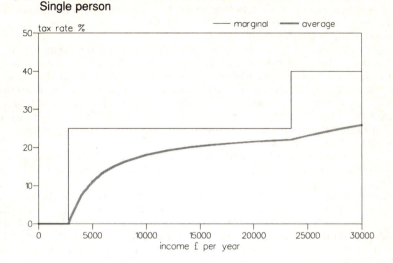

It should be noted that the term "progression" is sometimes defined in terms of the *marginal rate of tax*, or the amount that is paid on the *next* £1 of income. So that, in our example the marginal tax rate (in 1989) is 25 per cent for the person on £15,000 and 40 per cent for the person on £30,000. In this case it is true that the marginal tax rate rises with income, as shown on Chart 2.1, but this is not required for the definition of progression that we have adopted here. A progressive tax can have just one rate of tax above the exemption level: for example, if the higher rate were abolished the person on £30,000 would still pay a greater percentage of their income in tax (22.7 per cent). While we recommend in this Report that the marginal rates of income tax should rise with income, what we refer to as a *graduated* structure of rates, one could have a progressive system without such a structure.

One of the main reasons for our recommendation in Chapter 5 of a graduated rate structure is that this would increase the *degree* of progression. Chart 2.1 shows that the percentage collected in tax, after rising quite steeply, levels off at around 20 per cent for quite a range. By adopting a graduated structure of rates, rather than a single basic rate band, it is possible to make the initial rise less steep and for the proportion collected in tax to rise more evenly.

At the same time, it must be remembered that this method of assessing the degree of progression assumes that people actually pay the notional amount of tax used in these calculations. In practice, many people can claim reliefs against mortgage interest or pension contributions which will lower their average rate. Those with sources of income not taxed through PAYE may be able to lower further their effective rate of tax by making use of the advice offered by the tax avoidance industry. It is for this reason that it is important to consider the definition of the tax base and that in Chapter 7 we make recommendations for the broadening of the tax base.

Quantitative analysis of taxation often focusses on the *family*, treating as a unit a married couple and any dependent children. In our view, it is important to consider the distribution of income *within* the family, particularly that between men and women. The tax treatment of women is an area on which Labour has rightly focussed. The reform of income taxation and other taxes needs not just to ensure formal equality of treatment between men and women, but also to contribute positively to ensuring independence.

It is sometimes suggested that support for Labour requires the electorate to vote altruistically — and that altruism is out of fashion in Thatcherite Britain. It is however the case that many of the reforms advocated in this Report would benefit the large *majority* of the electorate. It is quite possible to design a revenue-neutral package of reforms such that there are at least three times as many gainers as losers. While the potential losers will no doubt be more vocal than the potential gainers, there will be a considerable degree of support for the reforms. We do not accept that people always act in their own self interest, and Labour can make a strong appeal to people's sense of fairness. But it does not need to rely on altruism. For over three-quarters of the electorate, voting Labour would be in their own interest if Labour were to follow policies along the lines recommended in this Report.

Objectives of taxation: incentives and disincentives

Debate about taxation has focussed on its *negative* aspects, but the Committee feels that these have received too much attention. Cuts in taxes may discourage work effort as much as increase it, as has been shown in empirical studies of decisions by individual workers. The less easily quantifiable aspects, like willingness to take responsibility or effort, may well be more affected by considerations such as morale than by narrow pecuniary calculations. Certainly nothing can be deduced from the fact that top salaries have increased greatly; this may be quite unrelated to any increase in productivity induced by tax changes. And the group for which the clearest evidence exists of disincentive effects — married women — may be as much affected by child care provisions and flexible employment opportunities as by marginal or average tax rates. As far as Britain's poor economic performance over the post-war period is concerned, taxation does not seem to have been a major contributory factor. International comparisons show that Britain is not, and has not been, a high tax country (see Chapter 3). There appears to be no clear link between levels of taxation and rates of economic growth.

Indeed it must not be forgotten that taxation may play a positive rather than a negative role in improving economic performance. The ability to exempt certain types of activity from taxation can provide a positive incentive, as has been the case with investment incentives under previous Labour Governments. The structure of National Insurance contribution rates may be set in such a way as to encourage the employment of groups disadvantaged in the labour market, whose full potential is not being realised. A number of European countries use tax concessions for child care as a means of helping women re-enter the labour force. The tax system could equally be used to encourage the acquisition of qualifications and training. Moreover, the tax system may be used to discourage activities which are regarded as socially harmful, environmental damage being the obvious example.

Where we do agree that taxation has been too important is the role which it has come to play in economic life, as is evidenced by the growth of the professional tax advice industry. This affects not so much the economic decisions themselves as the *form* in which people receive their income or hold their wealth. We believe that Labour should aim to reduce the role played by taxation so that it only plays a significant role in those cases where there is an explicit objective of public policy — like the opening up of employment opportunities or the encouragement of owner-occupation. We favour not a "level playing field" of the type espoused in the American tax reform, but one that is tilted in certain clearly specified and publicly announced directions. It would not be like the present situation where you discover sudden drops or are suddenly confronted with steep hills, depending on which path you choose, or on whose map you follow or — worse still — there is a general impression that others are coasting down-hill while you are faced with an uphill climb.

A particularly steep hill that is faced by low income families is the *poverty trap*. This is the situation where an increase in gross earnings leads to little or no increase in net income when account is taken of taxation and the withdrawal of means-tested benefits. This may be illustrated by the case of a man on £7,500 a year — about 60 per cent of average male earnings. He is liable to income tax and National Insurance contributions (NIC). On an additional £1 a week he is subject to tax of 25 per cent and NIC of 9 per cent, reducing the gain in net income to 66p. If he has two children aged 12 and 14 and savings below £3,000 then he is eligible for family credit on an income of up to some £9,000 a year in 1989/90, so that he will be in the situation of both paying income tax and receiving a means-tested benefit. This means that if he earns an extra £1 a week, the re-assessment of family credit will lead to its being reduced by 70 per cent of the gain in net income — or

$$0.7 \times 66p = 46.2p$$

So that the gain in net income falls to 19.8p, which implies that the marginal rate is 80.2 per cent. Nor is this the only way in which high marginal tax rates may arise. The family may be receiving housing benefit. If the man described above had been earning £6,000 a year, and there was no other family income apart from child benefit and family credit, and they paid rent of £28 per week and rates of £11, then a £1 a week rise in earnings would lead to a 16.8p reduction in housing benefit. The final marginal tax rate is then 97 per cent. From an extra £1 earned, the net gain is 3p.

The number affected by the poverty trap is relatively small — about

3 per cent of working family heads — but the same is true of the number facing high marginal rates at the top end of the scale, where a great deal of attention has been focussed. We shall therefore consider in later chapters the role of tax and social security reforms which can contribute to ensuring that low income families can do more to improve their circumstances by their own efforts. However, we should note here our general conclusion that the reform of *taxation* on its own can make only a limited contribution. The key to getting rid of the poverty trap is in the removal of means tested benefits with high withdrawal rates, particularly family credit.

The economic and social context

The reform of taxation has to be seen against the wider background of economic and social developments. Among the most important in the last few years which directly affect families are:

- widening inequality of pay;
- shift from wages to profits;
- increased owner-occupation;
- wider share ownership and receipt of investment income;
- increased self-employment;
- shift from manufacturing to service sector;
- more part-time work;
- increased reliance on private provision of pensions;
- reductions in state benefits and social insurance relative to earnings;
- widening regional disparities.

In some cases, we take these changes as part of the context within which policy has to be designed. In other cases, such as low pay and widening regional disparities, there are policies already agreed by Labour (such as a national minimum wage) which seek to reverse the trend of the 1980s.

In addition, there are longer-run trends in British society. These include:

- greater economic independence for women;
- changing and less durable patterns of marriage;
- earlier retirement;
- rapidly increasing numbers of the very old;
- more flexible employment relations.

In considering changes in, for instance, the tax treatment of husbands and wives, or the role of National Insurance contributions, we have tried to take account of these trends, with the aim of designing a tax system that is relevant to the mid-1990s.

One important set of changes which is taking place despite, rather than on account of the Government, is the growing effect of Europe on British economic and social life. Whatever the precise outcome of the proposals for 1992, there will undoubtedly be major changes. It is important that Labour *both* play an active role in ensuring that these changes are in accord with its — rather than the Government's — vision of the future *and* plan its policies so that they are consistent with the

Europe of the 1990s. The European Commission has proposed, as part of the progress to a common internal market, the approximation of VAT rates and the harmonisation of excise duties. More far-reaching would be measures to bring into line personal direct taxes and corporate taxes. In view of this, we have sought to make reference wherever possible to the European dimension of the different issues discussed — the issues of the tax base and of the tax unit being prime examples.

Policy in other areas: social security

In considering the proposals for the reform of taxation, it is essential that there be co-ordinated policy in these two areas. In important cases, tax allowances perform essentially the same function as social security benefits. This was recognised when child tax allowances and family allowances were combined to form child benefit, and the same applies for example to the age allowance. In this report we concentrate on taxation but make references to social security policy. When discussing the personal allowances in Chapter 6 we need to consider tax changes in conjunction with benefit changes. We make the working assumption for example that there will be an increase in child benefit and in the National Insurance retirement pension.

It is however not just the level but also the *structure* of social security benefits that is relevant. Labour's approach to social security is based firmly on *social insurance*. We have not considered in any detail the main alternative to social insurance, which is a basic income scheme based on the integration of income tax personal allowances and social security benefits. Rather than integration, what we are proposing amounts to the *co-ordination* of income tax and social insurance.

The social insurance approach is quite complementary to that put forward for income taxation in this Report. In particular, National Insurance is largely based on an independent assessment, which is in line with the proposed move to independence for taxation. The same is not true of the means-tested strategy of the Conservatives, where there is an evident tension between independence for taxation and the use of the family (or household) as the unit for assessing benefit. This has been demonstrated well by the poll tax. One of the main arguments used by its supporters was that the *individual* should pay for the local authority levels of spending for which he or she voted. But couples are to be jointly and severally liable for the payment of each other's tax and the rebate scheme is assessed on *family* income.

Conclusions

The primary objectives of the tax system should be to raise revenue for vital public services in a way that is fair and which attracts public confidence. Fairness means that each of us should be treated in an even-handed way and that those on low incomes should pay a smaller proportion of their income in tax than those who are higher paid. In addition, taxation should be designed as far as possible, to promote

Britain's economic performance, rather than undermine it; and we should seek to reduce the ways in which taxation may distort business decisions and choices people make about their lives. Labour's plans for taxation should be forward-looking through the 1990s, taking account of changing economic and social circumstances and of Britain's international responsibilities, including a wider role in the European Community.

Chapter 3

Sources of tax revenue

Tax structure in Britain

Taxation in Britain at present amounts to some 38 per cent of national income (GDP at market prices). By international standards, this puts Britain in about the middle of OECD countries — see Chart 3.1. Historically, the tax burden has been high in relation to the United States and to Japan, and it has been low in relation to Scandinavia and Benelux. Certainly, Britain has never been amongst the highest taxed countries in the OECD; and in this respect Labour's record in the past has been mis-represented. It was in much the same position under Denis Healey relative to other countries as under Nigel Lawson.

Chart 3.1: The tax burden in OECD countries
Taxes and social security contributions 1986

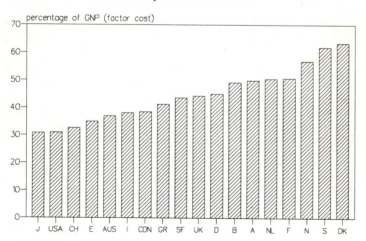

Key: J–Japan, USA–United States, CH–Switzerland, E–Spain, AUS–Australia, I–Italy, CDN–Canada, GR–Greece, SF–Finland, UK–United Kingdom, D–West Germany, B–Belgium, A–Austria, NL–Netherlands, F–France, N–Norway, S–Sweden, DK–Denmark

Chart 3.2: Tax ratio 1974/5 to 1989/90

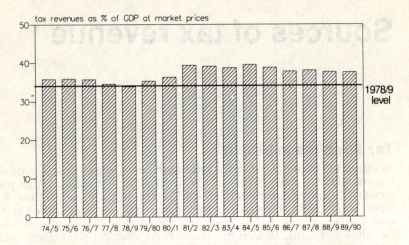

tax revenues as % of GDP at market prices

The percentage of tax in GDP at market prices in this Chart is lower than the percentage of tax in GNP at factor cost in Chart 3.1. This is because Chart 3.1 measures income excluding indirect taxes and subsidies whereas they are included in income in Chart 3.2. The GNP measure includes net property income from abroad, GDP does not.

The Conservative record too has been mis-represented. Despite the claims that they have reduced taxation, the tax ratio is higher than when they came to power — see Chart 3.2. While taxation is lower than in the early 1980s, it is still higher than in 1978/9, when it was only 34 per cent. Taxes have risen, not fallen, in relation to national output over the period Mrs Thatcher has been in office. The much trumpeted tax cuts of the Lawson years have not yet offset the tax increases which took place when Sir Geoffrey Howe was Chancellor.

The reason that the Conservatives have been able to convey the impression of tax cuts is that they have changed the *structure* of taxation and they have *redistributed* the tax burden. The taxes they have cut are more visible than those which they have increased; and higher income groups are paying less tax. What is less obvious is that other taxes have been increased and that the tax burden has been shifted towards the less well-off.

The tax structure in 1988/9 is shown in the pie chart (Chart 3.3). The segments shown separately indicate the taxes covered in the Report; they account for about 70 per cent of the total. The changes since 1978/9 in the proportions raised from different taxes include:

- income tax decreased from 34.6% in 1978/9 to 28.1% in 1988/9;
- VAT increased from 8.3% in 1978/9 to 15.1% in 1988/9;
- corporation tax increased from 4.1% in 1978/9 to 8.2% in 1988/9.

Chart 3.3: The tax structure in 1988/9

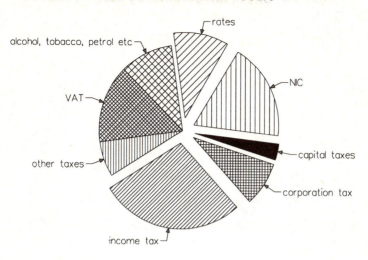

Three segments shown together indicate the taxes not covered in the Report.

The taxes that have grown as a proportion of total revenue include VAT, which has nearly doubled in significance, and corporation tax which has literally doubled. The increase in VAT rate in 1979 was certainly conspicuous, but the share of VAT has also been increased by a widening of the base and about a third of the 6.8 per cent increase has taken place surreptitiously in this form. This is partly because as the income distribution widens the proportion of spending by the better-off on zero-rated goods such as food gets smaller, but it is also partly because of the bringing into the tax base of zero-rated items, such as take-away food. This rise in VAT has been less noticed by the electorate than the almost equal fall in income tax. The rise in corporation taxes has also had little direct impact on voters.

In the case of income tax, receipts have fallen from a third of the total revenue in 1978/9 to little more than a quarter. The major element in the fall in income tax revenue has been the cut in the basic rate and its high political visibility has undoubtedly allowed the Government to create the impression that taxes have fallen overall and for everybody. The Government has focussed on the fact that the basic rate was 33 per cent when Labour left office and is now 25 per cent, but this gives a quite misleading impression. We recommend in Chapter 5 that the basic rate be abolished and replaced with a graduated structure, the rate of tax starting at a lower level than the Conservatives' basic rate and rising by steps. This will direct attention towards the amounts of tax that people actually pay, and here the Government's record is much less impressive and more divisive — see Chart 3.4 which shows the picture at different

Chart 3.4: Direct tax burdens by earnings levels

Single

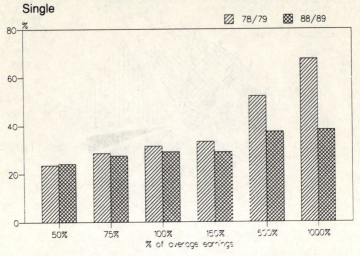

Married, both earning

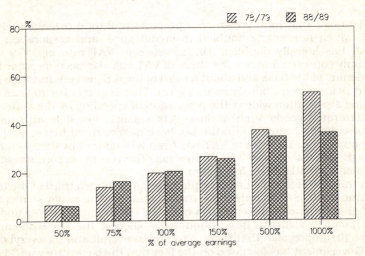

levels of earnings relative to the average for men paid at adult rates. The proportion of income paid in tax and National Insurance contributions (NIC) has certainly fallen at high earnings levels, as a result of the generosity to the rich in the 1988 Budget. For those on average earnings too there has been a fall, by 2.4 per cent for a single person. But this does not apply to those with half average earnings; and it must be remembered that even among the full-time employed, about 30 per cent of women earn less than half the average earnings of men. Nor does it apply to a couple where both have average earnings, as is shown in the lower part of Chart 3.4. Not everyone has benefitted from the Conservative cuts in direct taxation.

The redistribution of the tax burden does not just affect direct taxes; the switch from direct to indirect taxes has also had distributional implications. The extent to which indirect tax increases have offset direct tax reductions at different levels of earnings is illustrated in Chart 3.5. At average earnings and 1½ times average earnings there is little overall change for single people. But for two-earner couples, there has been a rise, especially for those on ¾ average earnings. (The figures here cover VAT, petrol and excise taxes, but there is no reason to believe that other taxes omitted from the calculations, such as corporation tax, would reverse the picture.)

This redistribution of the tax burden by the Conservatives is without any justification. Why should those on 75 per cent of average earnings now pay nearly as large a fraction of their income in tax as those earning double that amount? In our view the tax system overall should be progressive, with those on higher incomes contributing a significantly larger proportion in taxation. The return to a more progressive tax system is important for two reasons. First, the problem of poverty in Britain will be eased by the transfer of part of the tax burden from those on low incomes towards those better able to afford to contribute to public services. Secondly, there is the relative tax burden on different income groups, where we believe that the proportionate contribution should rise steadily with income. We are concerned about the whole pattern of tax burdens.

The aim of our proposals is therefore to make the tax system progressive in its overall impact. In this Report we are focussing on only part of the picture, but it is clear that a key step in securing overall progression is to reverse the redistribution of the direct tax burden.

Conclusions

Under the Conservatives tax overall has risen, and there has been a redistribution in the tax burden, with the direct tax system (income tax and National Insurance contributions) becoming less progressive. The proportion paid in tax now rises markedly less with the level of income. We believe that under Labour's tax policy the direct tax system should be made more progressive. With the present structure of indirect taxation, it is necessary that *direct* taxes be made more progressive, in order to secure a progressive overall distribution of the tax burden.

Chart 3.5: Direct and indirect tax burdens by earnings level

Single

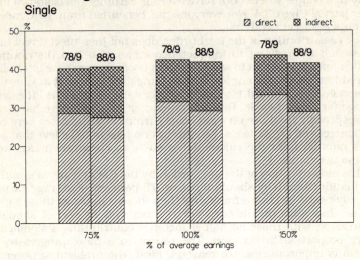

Married, both earning

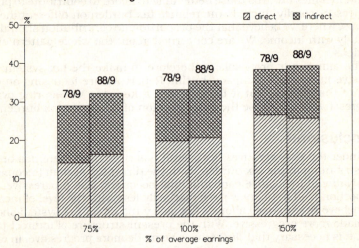

Chapter 4

Choice of tax base

Income as a tax base

We are judging the progression of the tax system in terms of income, but before examining proposals for its reform we have to ask why income should be the basis for taxation and what indeed we mean by "income".

The definition of income that we adopt here is the comprehensive definition that includes everything that people receive, or which accrues to them, and which adds to their potential spending power. We agree with Lord Kaldor and his colleagues who wrote in the Minority Report to the 1955 Royal Commission on the Taxation of Profits and Income that

> *"no concept of income can be really equitable that stops short of the comprehensive definition which embraces all receipts which increase an individual's command over the use of society's scarce resources"* (page 355).

Or, more concretely, it is the sum of
(i) the market value of rights exercised in consumption, plus
(ii) change in the real value of assets during the period in question.

There are four aspects of this "ideal" definition which require comment. The first is that it is *potential* and not *actual* spending power that is relevant. The base is income and not expenditure (which would exclude item (ii) above). The question whether we should move to an expenditure tax base is discussed in the next section of this chapter. The second is that it relates to a specified period, being a flow rather than a stock measure, although it has often been argued that the stock of wealth would provide an alternative basis for taxation. Normally the period is taken to be the tax year, although in some cases it may be argued that the relevant period is the whole of a person's lifetime, a point to which we return in Chapter 9 when discussing capital transfers. Thirdly, the change in the value of assets is measured in *real terms*. In the case of capital gains, the present British system makes such an allowance for inflation and hence taxes real gains (or losses), but in the case of interest and dividend income no adjustment is made for inflation. According to the "ideal" definition, a person holding money in a bank account on which interest accrues at a rate of 12 per cent should only be taxed on the excess of this amount over the rate of inflation. This is a point which we take up below. Fourthly, the change in the value of assets is that which has *accrued*, not that which is *realised*. Unlike the present tax treatment of capital gains, where tax on capital gains is postponed until the date at which the asset is sold, the "ideal" definition treats as income the gains accruing on assets which the person continues to own (just like interest accruing in a bank account). The difference between an accruals basis and a realisations basis is taken up in Chapter 9.

The comprehensive definition of income provides a benchmark against which we can judge the case in terms of equity for changes in the actual tax base. It is relevant to both *horizontal* equity and *vertical* equity. It is clear for example that fringe benefits, insofar as they provide the equivalent of consumption, should be included in full. Not to do so would be horizontally inequitable to the person who receives all his or her remuneration in cash, and it would be vertically inequitable to the extent that fringe benefits are received disproportionately by the better-off. Lump-sum payments by pension funds should be as much part of the tax base as are regular payments of pensions. The income which an owner-occupier receives in kind from the occupation of the house counts just as much as if he rents out the house and receives cash income from the tenant. As it was put by the CBI,

> *"in principle the deemed consumption benefits from housing should be taxed (as was the notional "income" from owner-occupation under Schedule A until 1963)"* (Tax — Time for Change, *CBI, 1985, page 111).*

There may of course be reasons of efficiency why we wish to depart from the comprehensive tax base. There may be activities which a Labour Government wishes to encourage and which are best stimulated by exemption of the income from taxation. It is possible that the deemed income from owner-occupation comes in this category. There may be practical considerations which mean that no satisfactory method can be devised of taxing certain types of income. This may again apply to the deemed income from owner-occupation. At the same time, departures on efficiency grounds from the comprehensive base have equity costs. It is horizontally inequitable that owner-occupiers pay less tax than tenants who have invested in another form. It may well be vertically inequitable in that owner-occupiers tend to be better off. A judgement on the extent of the tax base must balance these considerations. In general, as in the housing example, there will be many complex issues involved in that judgement and it will not always be possible to follow consistent principles. In Chapter 7, we consider a number of such cases.

Money versus real return to capital

The "ideal" definition would treat as investment income only the excess of the money return over that required to maintain the real value. Suppose for example that an asset appreciates at the rate of inflation, then there is no real capital gain to be taxed. Allowance is made for this in that capital gains are indexed for tax purposes, but no such adjustment is made for investment income in other forms. If a person keeps money in the building society and earns 10 per cent interest, then the real return is the difference between 10 per cent and the rate of inflation. If inflation is 6 per cent, then for each £100 the person needs to add £6 each year to maintain the real value of the account, so that the real return is only £4. However, tax is charged on the full £10.

In principle, the tax treatment of investment income should be converted to a real basis by allowing indexation of all assets and correspondingly only allowing real interest for tax deductions, so that the amount of mortgage interest relief would be reduced. (Of course, one should only allow real interest to be deducted since, if real receipts were taxed but money interest deductible, this would create a "money machine", tax being saved each time the money goes round.) Overall this would reduce the tax burden on investment income, and it is interesting that this step has not been taken by the present Government, nor indeed been extensively discussed. There are two obvious reasons. The first is the loss of revenue, which would be very substantial and would mean a rise in the tax rate on earned income. The second is the administrative complexity. In theory at least, indexation would require information on the timing of each transaction into and out of an account so that the appropriate inflation factor could be applied; in practice, any administrative rule would only approximate the correct inflation adjustment and would give scope for manipulation. It would also pose the Inland Revenue unenviable problems in explaining the rationale for the adjustment and its operation. A third consideration which weighed with us is that it is not evident that the distributional consequences would be in line with our goal of increasing the effective degree of progression. We do not therefore recommend that any indexation be applied to investment income in general.

Expenditure or income tax

One of the most important potential departures from the income tax base would be the total exemption of savings, which would convert the income tax into an expenditure tax. The argument for an expenditure tax base rather than an income tax base may in fact be made on either efficiency or equity grounds.

As far as efficiency is concerned, one of the most powerful arguments for an expenditure tax is that the present British income tax already contains major elements of an expenditure tax: the treatment of pension funds, for example, is much closer to an expenditure tax than to an income tax base. The introduction of a fully-fledged expenditure tax would simply recognise that we have gone a long way in this direction and would "level the playing field" by extending an expenditure tax-treatment to all forms of savings rather than the present privileged class. This would, it is argued, secure "fiscal neutrality". And, since we have already moved a substantial way in the direction of an expenditure tax, the transition would be relatively straightforward.

This argument is attractive, but is open to two major objections. The first is that Labour may not want a level playing field. There may be certain types of saving that it seeks to encourage, in which case an

25

expenditure tax treatment may be appropriate for these but not for other forms of saving. Secondly, if the playing field is to be levelled it is not clear that it should be in the direction of an expenditure tax rather than an income tax.

What inherent advantages does the expenditure tax possess? One claim that is often made is that an income tax, by putting a wedge between the before-tax return to savings and the after-tax return, distorts decisions about savings; and to the extent that certain types of savings receive privileged treatment, it distorts the *pattern* of savings. The move to an expenditure tax basis, it is suggested, would eliminate these distortions, and lead to more efficient decisions about savings. A related, but distinct, argument is that the income tax discourages personal savings, with the reduction in the after-tax return leading people to save less than with an expenditure tax.

Neither of these arguments is fully convincing. While the expenditure tax would not put a wedge between the before- and after-tax rates of return, the rate of tax would almost certainly have to be higher, on account of the overall tax base being smaller (since total personal expenditure is typically less than total personal income). This means that the tax on, say, earned incomes would have to be higher, and hence there would be greater distortion of decisions about work. (It is also the case that the saving decision would be distorted by expectations of a change in the rate of expenditure tax — see below.) The expenditure tax base is not unambiguously superior. Secondly, it is not clear that a switch to the expenditure tax would raise the level of savings. *A priori*, savers may react in either direction. The person with a specific savings target may save more rather than less on account of the income tax. In practice, the introduction of an expenditure tax would act like a rise in the interest rate, and the substantial rise in real interest rates in recent years does not seem to have generated a large rise in savings.

The efficiency arguments are not therefore ones that we find sufficiently compelling to accept the expenditure tax base. Moreover, the international aspects of tax policy formation have to be taken into account. There is no doubt that if Britain switched unilaterally to an expenditure tax base then financial relations with countries retaining an income tax base would become more complicated. There would, at the very least, have to be measures to prevent people benefitting from the tax-deductibility of saving in Britain and then moving abroad with their accumulated assets and dis-saving under an income tax regime. The proposals of the Meade Committee in 1978 for an expenditure tax envisaged that there would have to be special provisions to prevent such avoidance. However, the moves which have been taken since then in the direction of harmonisation in Europe mean that such provisions would be difficult, if not impossible, to implement. The single market would in effect rule out an exit tax which would be the only way for the UK, under an expenditure tax regime, to prevent savings being spent elsewhere in Europe.

On equity grounds it is argued that we should be concerned with what people take out of the economic system, or what they spend, rather than what they put in, which is related to their income. As it is put in the celebrated quotation from Hobbes,

"what reason is there, that he which laboureth much, and sparing the fruits of his labour, consumeth little, should be more charged, than he that living idly, getteth little and spendeth all he gets?" (Leviathan, *Chapter XXX*)

As far as horizontal equity is concerned, much of the force of this quotation comes from the "idleness" and here the change in tax base would make no difference: extra leisure would be taxed under neither an income tax nor an expenditure tax. Where the case may be stronger is that it may be easier under an expenditure tax than under an income tax to exempt that part of the return to capital which is simply keeping up with inflation, in the sense that it is not necessary with an expenditure tax to measure *real* incomes. On the other hand, the vertical equity arguments may favour the income tax, given our objective of increasing the effective degree of progression. In principle, any desired degree of progression could be achieved by an expenditure tax. In practice, the tax rates would have to be higher, and to rise more steeply, in order to reproduce just the existing distribution of the tax burden, and this is likely to encounter political opposition. In our view, political considerations would limit the feasible degree of redistribution under an expenditure tax to a greater extent than under the broader income tax base. This may indeed be one of the reasons why it finds support in other political parties.

A second version of the equity argument is that we should judge the taxable capacity of a person in terms of the whole lifetime, taxing the amounts received from "outside" whether in the form of earnings or transfers of capital, but not taxing the income which arises because the person decides to postpone consumption. A person should be taxed on all lifetime receipts, whether from wages or from inheritances or from gifts, but allowed freedom to re-arrange consumption without having to bear tax on the interest earned by deferring consumption. Whatever the intrinsic merits of this lifetime approach, it is not one that has attracted political support, perhaps because it assumes a stability in the tax regime which no country has yet managed to achieve. If the rate of expenditure tax varied from one government to the next then there could be considerable variation in the lifetime tax burden across individuals, otherwise equally placed, on account of differences in their timing of spending.

The consequences of changing tax rates are in fact too often overlooked in the debate. One of the features of the expenditure tax is that it allows more flexibility to the individual taxpayer to decide when to pay tax. Under the income tax base there is a determinate date at which tax is due. With an expenditure tax, taxpayers — or at least better-off taxpayers — can, by increasing the amount saved, postpone tax liability. The expectation of tax changes will then have the effect of distorting savings decisions — destroying the fiscal "neutrality" claimed for the expenditure tax.

Expectations of tax changes may similarly create problems under an expenditure tax for a Labour Chancellor. Despite the experience of the last decade, some people may be taken in by the claim that taxes under the Conservatives would be lower, so that a Labour Chancellor may find that the tax base is seriously reduced as taxpayers "speculate" on the return of the Conservatives. There could be cash flow problems for a Labour Government.

Conclusions

These considerations led us to the view that the base for personal direct taxation should be income rather than expenditure, while recognising that there may be principled reasons — to do with economic efficiency or administrative feasibility — for departing from the strict comprehens-ive benchmark. The way in which we propose that this can be translated into practice is the subject of Chapter 7.

Chapter 5

A progressive rate structure for income taxation

The case for a more progressive income tax

The extent to which direct taxes have over time become less progressive may be seen by comparing the situation after the April 1989 Budget with that thirty years ago — going back to an earlier 13-year period of Conservative rule. In April 1959 the average tax rate of a person on average male earnings was lower than in 1989 — by some 5 percentage points. But what is striking is that the *relative* tax burdens were very different:

	income tax burden	
	then (1959)	now (1989)
person on ⅔ average earnings	10%	17% (up 7%)
person on 2 x average earnings	23%	25% (up 2%)
person on 10 x average earnings	48%	37% (down 11%)

All calculations are for a single person

The tax burden on the person earning twice average earnings used to be *more than double* that of a person on ⅔ of the average. Now it is less than half as much again. (It should be noted that about a quarter of men, and 60 per cent of women, earn less than two thirds of the male average; and about 4 per cent of men and 0.5 per cent of women earn more than double the male average.) Put another way, the tax burden on the person with ⅔ average earnings has risen by 7 percentage points, compared with 2 percentage points for the person earning three times as much. And the income tax burden on top earners has fallen quite dramatically: the average tax rate of those on ten times average earnings was 48 per cent and is now 37 per cent.

Chart 5.1: Average tax rates and income levels
1959 and 1984/5

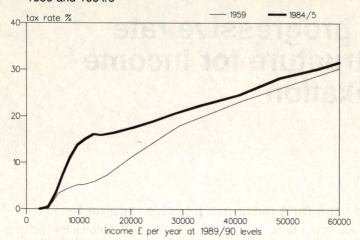

Incomes for both 1959 and 1984/5 are approximately adjusted to
1989/90 levels using changes in average taxable income

These calculations are hypothetical ones, and do not relate to real
families with their diversity of circumstances. This diversity of circumstances is relevant since it affects the extent to which they can take
advantage of other tax reliefs (such as earned income relief in 1959 or
mortgage interest relief) and thus reduce their tax burden. Chart 5.1
shows the average income tax rate actually paid by families at different
total income levels, as estimated by the Central Statistical Office on the
basis of information from income tax records and other sources. The
most up-to-date figures currently available are those for 1984/5, the
annual publication of these statistics having been one of the casualties
of the cuts in official statistics. (For convenience, the income levels have
been adjusted to 1989/90 levels.) They do not therefore show the impact
of the reduction in top rates to 40 per cent.

Comparing 1984/5 with 1959, we can see that the big increase in the
tax burden has taken place in the middle range of incomes, which is
from about three-quarters to one and a half times the average family
income, with the widest gap being at the level of average income. By the
time one gets to twice average income, the curves are much closer, the
increase in the average tax burden being much less at higher income
levels. The changes up to 1984/5 served therefore to accentuate the
redistribution of the tax burden, and there can be little doubt that figures
for 1989/90 would show an even more marked move in this direction.
While holding no particular brief for the Chancellorship of Mr Heathcoat
Amory, in our view the distribution of the income tax burden 30 years

ago was a fairer one than that under present day Conservatives.

In our view, a reduction in the tax burden on the lowest paid is desirable on grounds of vertical equity. While the help that Labour can provide to low income families will depend particularly on improvements in benefits, and on the opening of pathways out of poverty, the income tax can be recast to reduce the extent of deductions from their incomes. At the same time, our concern is not solely with those right at the bottom. Those somewhat up from the bottom but still in the lower half of the income distribution — on whom the burden has increased particularly severely — are, in our judgement, bearing more than their fair share of the direct tax burden. We do not believe that a tax structure is fair if, as at present, a person on ⅔ average earnings pays as much as 17 per cent in income tax when a person earning three times that amount pays 25 per cent.

In this chapter we describe how we would seek to make the income tax more progressive. One important difference between the income tax structure of 1959 and that of 1989 is that there were then four income tax rates (on earned incomes) of 7 per cent, 16.5 per cent, 24 per cent and 30 per cent (all percentages rounded) before one got to the higher (surtax) rates. Our main recommendation is that we should return to a graduated rate structure, but before that we consider an alternative approach.

Raising the basic rate to finance a higher tax threshold

The present British rate structure consists of the two rates (the basic rate of 25 per cent and the higher rate of 40 per cent) and the associated thresholds. The structure could be made more progressive by raising the basic rate and using the additional revenue to take families out of the tax net.

Increasing the basic rate and using the revenue to increase personal allowances would take out of tax a sizeable number of families, but it is the middle income groups which would show the largest net gains. The gain in the middle would certainly contribute to making the tax structure more progressive, since it would reduce the burden on those who have suffered from the historical shift away from progression. An increase in the tax threshold would reduce the number of lower income people who were taxpayers which would be progressive in itself. At the same time, the scope for redistribution of the tax burden using simply the basic rate is limited. In effect the tax schedule "pivots" about average incomes, with people immediately above losing from the change. We may want to "tilt" the distribution of the tax burden less sharply about this level of income and this is not possible with the limited instruments of the threshold and the basic rate. There is not sufficient flexibility. Put another way, there would be a sizeable proportion of losers with this kind of reform; and we would hope to be able to reduce this number with a more flexible set of tax rates.

Nor are increases in the tax threshold alone an effective way of dealing with the problem of the poverty trap. This may be seen from the fact that, even without the 25 per cent basic rate, the marginal tax rate is 9 per cent NIC plus 63.7 per cent withdrawal of family credit (70 per cent x 0.91), making 72.7 per cent. Removing families from the tax net is not therefore in itself enough to ensure that their marginal tax rate falls below 70 per cent. The only way in which increases in the tax threshold can help is by raising net incomes and hence floating people off family credit altogether. It is clear however that this would require a very large increase in the personal allowances.

Finally, there can be little doubt that the rise in the basic rate would provide powerful campaigning material for the other parties. "Back to 33p in the £" would be a valid and effective depiction of Labour's policy, and it would be hard to counter-attack. On account of this political drawback, and the considerations already discussed, we have decided that this is not the route to follow.

A graduated rate structure

Our basic proposal for income tax is to replace the basic rate by a sequence of graduated rates, beginning below the present basic rate and increasing by steps to a maximum tax rate of 50 per cent. In this we concur with Labour's Policy Review. This approach would defuse the political charge of the basic rate. A wide basic rate band has administrative advantages, as discussed in Chapter 12, allowing the collection of tax at source with a minimum of adjustments for individual taxpayers. However, as argued there, it is possible to envisage an administrative scheme which allows for the introduction of a graduated rate structure. Other countries have operated such graduated rate structures. In France for example the rates begin at 5 per cent and rise by 5 per cent steps. In West Germany, the marginal rates from 1990 will rise linearly from 19 per cent to 53 per cent.

It is essential to our proposals that the initial rate of tax should represent a reduction over the basic rate inherited from the Conservatives. No doubt the Chancellor hopes that he will be able to reduce the basic rate below 25 per cent before the next election. If he were to do so, then by the same token we could reduce the proposed rate structure, but we do not allow for this possibility here. The graduated rate structure should therefore be compared with the present 25 per cent and 40 per cent rates.

As we have stressed, abandoning the constraints of the long basic rate band opens up great flexibility in structure — this is the particular advantage of moving to graduation. Examples to illustrate what would be possible include the following sets of rates:
- a "four rate" version of 20%, 36%, 41% and 50%;
- a "six rate" version of 15%, 22.5%, 30%, 37.5%, 45% and 50%.

Other examples could be chosen and have been suggested by, among others, the Treasury and Civil Service Committee Sub-committee in 1983. The effect of this type of schedule is to allow a more gradual progression of the tax system, reducing the burden on the majority of taxpayers, and recouping for those at the top the unjustified windfall they enjoyed in the 1988 Budget. In the case of the four-rate version, the rate of 20 per cent would become payable on income in excess of the personal allowances, up to the end of the band. In order to bring this out more clearly, we propose that the allowance be converted to a zero rate band. This would have the effect of giving a cash credit, dependant on the initial rate of tax but equal in value to all taxpayers, rather than a tax threshold whose value depends on the person's marginal tax rate. Under the current system of allowances, tax is paid by a single person on income in excess of £2,785 per year. The cash value of this allowance is £2,785 x 25 per cent for a basic rate taxpayer — £13.39 per week; to a higher rate taxpayer it is worth £2,785 x 40 per cent — £21.42 per week. If this allowance were converted into a zero rate band, it would have the same cash value to all taxpayers. Any increase in the zero rate band would not automatically provide greater benefit to higher rate taxpayers. The higher rate thresholds could be set and uprated independently of the zero rate band, the taxable income they applied to being always the person's total income less the zero rate band. As discussed in the next chapter, the zero rate band would be significantly larger than the present single personal allowance.

Consequential on the introduction of a graduated structure would be other changes in the income tax. The withholding rate of tax charged on investment income (for example building society or bank interest) would have to be determined, and this aspect is discussed further in later chapters. The rate of imputation for corporation tax is discussed in Chapter 10. Mortgage interest relief at source would be allowed at a single rate, and we recommend in Chapter 7 that this be the full extent of the relief, so that no adjustments would be necessary on this account for those paying higher rates of tax.

Incentives and marginal tax rates

We earlier pointed out that increases in the tax threshold alone were not an effective way of dealing with the poverty trap, which is essentially the result of means testing in the social security system. Changes to the tax system can only ameliorate the problem to a limited extent.

If we examine the effect of the graduated rates on marginal tax rates more generally, there are undoubtedly going to be increases for a sizeable fraction of taxpayers, even though they will pay less tax. This applies both to the new higher rate bands above 40 per cent and to the intermediate rates which exceed 25 per cent. But there are also going to be those whose marginal tax rate is reduced, and they are likely to be a majority. This applies particularly to married women, where employment decisions may be more sensitive to tax rates.

Conclusions

In our view a graduated rate structure offers an effective approach to making the income tax more progressive and to securing a fairer distribution of the tax burden.

Chapter 6

Personal allowances: the tax treatment of married couples, single parents, children and the elderly

Introduction

The British income tax through its system of personal allowances reduces the tax burden on married couples, single parents and the elderly, relative to the taxes paid by a single person without dependants and of working age. In this chapter we examine these additional personal allowances and child benefit (which replaced child tax allowances). We have to ask first whether we accept that these groups merit special consideration. Should their net income, other things equal, be higher than for the single worker without dependants? We have then to consider whether such help is best provided through the tax system rather than, say, through improvements in social security benefits. Single parents may, for example, receive One Parent Benefit.

The tax treatment of married couples will of course be affected by the changes due to come into force in April 1990 (which were announced by Mr Lawson in the 1988 Budget). After outlining the Lawson proposals, we go on to argue that Labour should adopt a policy of total independence in the tax treatment of husbands and wives, this being the only one appropriate for the 21st century.

Tax treatment of married couples: the 1990 changes

There are three main principles which underlie the case for the independent taxation of husbands and wives:

1. The tax system should neither encourage nor discourage marriage — married people should be treated in the same way as two single people.
2. Men and women should be treated in the same way for tax purposes.
3. Within marriage, the tax of one spouse should not depend on the income of the other.

Acceptance of these principles means that the married couple as a unit has no role in taxation and that, in particular, the amount of tax paid depends on who receives the income. This is in contrast to a system, like that in France, where a couple is taxed on their total income; this violates principle (3) and may, depending on the tax schedule, violate principle (1). One important consequence of independence is, however, that we have to monitor transfers of income between spouses. In addition it should be remembered that we do not start from a "level playing field" between the sexes. Equal treatment of men and women in tax matters does not necessarily promote equality and it may be that the tax system has a role to play in helping women towards genuine economic independence as well as a theoretical independence in their tax affairs.

None of the principles (1), (2) or (3) hold under the current (1989/90) system. Under this system, all income is treated as belonging to the husband, which clearly violates the second principle. A woman loses on marriage virtually all independence in her tax affairs. The husband receives a higher allowance than a single person (married man's allowance, or MMA). (If his income is less than this allowance, his wife's income may be set against it, since it is considered to be his income.) In addition the wife has an earned income allowance, equal in size to the single person's allowance, which she may use to set against earned income. This means that a two-earner couple within the basic rate band (see below for the case where higher rates are payable) pay less tax than two single persons with the same earnings (by the value of the excess of the MMA over the single allowance), and hence this violates the first principle. At the same time, all investment income of the wife is taxed at her husband's marginal rate, thus violating the third principle. Furthermore, she has no privacy in her tax affairs as all correspondence is carried out between her tax office and her husband.

Couples may elect to have the wife's earnings taxed separately (at her own marginal rate) at the cost of losing the extra married man's allowance. For separate election to be worthwhile, the tax that would be paid at the higher rate without election, but is only paid at the basic rate, has to be more than the extra value of the MMA to the husband. It is therefore of advantage to couples with a sizeable total income (over £30,511 in 1989/90) with the wife earning a substantial amount. This provision does not fully ensure symmetry, since it applies only to earned income. (Earnings election is different from separate assessment which is a means of dividing the tax bill between spouses.)

In response to widespread dissatisfaction with the present system, the Government has announced changes to take effect from April 1990. Referred to as "independent taxation", the 1990 changes will not in fact meet the three principles set out above, notably on account of the retention of the married man's allowance in the guise of the married couple's allowance (MCA). The MCA is not strictly equivalent to the excess of the MMA over the single allowance, but provides married couples with an *additional* personal allowance over and above the personal allowances each receives individually. At 1989/90 levels the MCA would be equal to £1,590: ie £4,375 (the MMA) minus £2,785 (the single allowance).

The 1990 changes may be seen as extending the separate election case to all couples. It does so by removing the penalty of losing the MMA (now the MCA) and by allowing separate election for all of the wife's income including investment income. There will be full personal allowances for all women just as for single persons. At the same time the MCA means that a couple will still pay less tax than two single persons with the same incomes. The first principle is therefore not satisfied.

Despite its neutral name, the married couple's allowance is to be allowable to the husband in the first instance and only transferable to the wife — at his request — where the husband's income does not exceed the single allowance plus MCA. Husbands and wives will not therefore be treated symmetrically, so that the second principle is not satisfied.

The 1990 changes mean that the income of a wife will no longer be treated as that of her husband. At the same time the tax paid by the wife will not be totally independent of the income of the husband. This is again because of the MCA. If the husband's income is below the sum of the single allowance and the MCA, then part or all of the allowance may be transferred, reducing the wife's tax bill. The third principle of independence is therefore violated.

The Lawson 1990 measures satisfy therefore none of the three principles. Nor will they have large distributional effects. There are in fact four main ways in which a couple will gain from the Lawson scheme. The first are couples who currently elect to have separate taxation of the wife's earnings. Under the 1990 proposals, tax will be paid by each spouse as at present, but the husband will now retain the benefit of the MCA, which is worth £7.64 per week at the basic rate and £12.23 for higher rate payers in 1989/90. By definition, it is only better-off couples who gain from this. The second way in which a couple may gain is if the wife receives a Category B pension (one based on her husband's contributions rather than her own). This would be taxed as his income under the current system. From 1990, her pension will be taxed as her income and will be set against her own allowance. Assuming she has not already used her allowance against earnings, she will gain some £6 per week which is the tax paid on a standard Category B pension by a basic rate tax payer. The third way in which a couple may gain is if they are both over 65 and both receive the age allowance under the new system. We consider the tax treatment of the elderly in a later section of this chapter.

The fourth effect of the reform occurs where the wife has unearned income. Under the current system, this can only be set against her husband's allowance. Under the new scheme, the wife will have her own personal allowance which she can set against any of her income. This will mean that in cases where the wife has unearned income, couples will gain if:

- the wife does not currently earn as much as her earned income allowance, or
- her unearned income plus the income of her husband is currently greater than the higher rate threshold.

Furthermore, there will also be an incentive for couples to re-arrange their assets between them so that their unearned income is set against their two allowances so as to minimise the income and capital gains taxes they pay.

There will in addition be some losers from the Lawson proposals. These include couples where the wife is the "breadwinner". Currently they can use all of the MMA as well as her earned income allowance, but under the 1990 proposals the total will be restricted to the single allowance plus the MCA, which gives a total only equal to the MMA. There will be transitional protection in such cases to ensure that there are no cash losses.

While it is not true that all those who stand to gain from Lawson's proposals are in the highest income brackets, the bulk of the gain does go to better-off couples. This certainly applies to those currently choosing separate election. It is also likely to apply to the disaggregation of investment income. Many people with small amounts of savings choose to place them in building societies or bank deposit accounts where the income is taxed at source. This tax is deducted before payment regardless of the status of the saver.

Genuine independence

It is Labour policy that the taxation of husbands and wives should be based on full independence. The Lawson proposals fall significantly short of achieving this objective. As we have seen, none of the three principles (1), (2) and (3) would be met. A man's tax bill will still fall on marriage. It will still be lower than that of his wife with the same earnings. For the couple to make best use of the MCA they must still find out about each other's financial affairs. Labour's response should be to introduce a genuinely independent system in which men and women are treated in the same way and in which tax liabilities are fully independent of marital status. Both partners in a marriage should have the right to complete privacy over information concerning their income, savings and other capital.

In choosing fully independent taxation, the Committee is not just following Labour Party policy. It has also considered the implications for personal taxation of increasing international mobility of labour and, particularly, the establishment of the single European market. It will not be uncommon for husbands and wives to work on different sides of the Channel and hence to be faced with different tax regimes. Although technically the resulting tax problems are soluble by residence rules and double taxation treaties, there is no doubt that these situations will be made considerably easier by full independence.

The central problem with the Lawson proposals is the retention of the married couple's allowance (MCA). The Committee recommends that there should be a significant increase in the single person's allowance (SPA), while the MCA is reduced in such a way as to leave the total of the SPA and MCA unchanged. If this policy is pursued in successive Budgets, the MCA would be phased out. The fact that the MCA would be reduced £ for £ with the increase in the single allowance, means that couples would either be left in the same cash position or enjoy an improvement (where both benefitted from the increased single allowance). An increase in the SPA has the advantage of reducing the number of less well off taxpayers.

The Committee considered whether the MCA should be split between husband and wife as a transitional arrangement while it is being phased out. The two halves of the extra allowance would be transferable in either direction where one partner did not have taxable income sufficient to make use of the allowance. The main advantage of dividing the MCA in the first instance would be that it would constitute a clear and immediate but low-cost move towards equality between the sexes. There would be some extra revenue arising from the fact that more husbands are in the higher rate band, against which would have to be set any additional administrative cost involved in more frequent transfer decisions being made, and any loss of revenue from differences in the degree of re-arrangement of investment income. Within couples, there may be some shift in tax burden from wives to husbands. On the other hand, there would be pressures to retain this remaining tax advantage to marriage and the numbers who might see themselves as losing from the phasing-out of the extra allowance would be greater by the number of taxpayer wives. Either of these options would have advantages. For reasons of simplicity, the rest of this chapter assumes that the transitional splitting of the MCA does not take place.

Fully independent taxation — like the Lawson proposals — will provide tax savings to couples with investment income. This is a matter which the Committee has taken into account when considering the treatment of investment income, where it proposes more effective taxation (see Chapters 7 and 8).

The interaction needs to be considered between these proposals for the tax treatment of couples and those for a graduated rate structure in Chapter 5. In particular, it is much more likely under a graduated structure than under the current system that husband and wife would be on different marginal rates. Transfer of investment income (and self-employment income) between spouses would therefore be potentially more important. Of course, it is in principle possible that other pairs or groups of individuals might transfer assets to gain maximum advantage from personal allowances and rate bands but it is mainly the institution of marriage that at present makes this particular transfer appear to be a secure proposition. However, with the increasing probability of divorce, and the way in which property is divided on divorce, it may be that the risks involved by the wealthier partner giving away capital are perceived as too great. The scale of re-allocation may not be very large although it will undoubtedly be the case that it will be the better advised that will make the most of the new situation. To the extent that this corresponds to a genuine equalisation of assets within marriage, then this may be welcomed. Indeed, if women have lower tax rates on account of their lower earnings, then there will be a definite incentive for husbands to transfer more than half the assets, and in this respect independent taxation will have a desirable effect on family behaviour. At the same time, consideration needs to be given to the conditions under which income can be transferred and to ensuring that it corresponds to genuine transfers. We welcome the steps taken in the 1989 Finance Act to disregard for tax purposes gifts which are conditional or where the donor has the right to get the asset back in the future, and to limit the use of trusts, although it is not clear that they are particularly effective.

In the immediate future there is also the issue of the MCA and its relation to the graduated structure. Transfer of the MCA would be limited to situations where one person had income below the level of the single allowance plus MCA (so that it could not be switched simply to take advantage of different marginal rates). But the cost of the wife increasing her earnings above the single threshold would depend on the marginal rate paid by her husband, which could be greater under the graduated structure. There may then be undesirable pressure on wives to curtail their paid work. We recommend that the MCA be given in the form of an additional zero rate band, with the initial rate band being reduced by a corresponding amount. This limits the benefit from the MCA to the initial rate, so that it would be worth the same to all taxpayers and there would be no fiscal advantage in the wife not making use of her allowance.

Single parents

At present the tax system provides help to single parents in the form of the additional personal allowance (APA), which means that they receive the same total allowance as a married man. This addition is worth £7.64 a week in 1989/90 if they are basic rate taxpayers, £12.23 a week if they are higher rate taxpayers, and nothing if they have a taxable income below the single allowance.

Under the 1990 proposals this is to be retained. (The one change announced in the 1988 Budget was that two co-habiting but unmarried parents can no longer from April 1989 claim two additional personal allowances.)

The continuation of the APA at a time when the MCA is being phased out would be inconsistent with the principle that the tax paid should be independent of marital status. The Committee is of the view that help to single parents is best provided through the social security system, not least because it helps those whose earnings are too low for them to get full benefit from the APA. (The social security benefits specifically for single parents include the widowed mother's allowance, the income support premium, housing benefit premium and One Parent Benefit). It therefore recommends that the APA be phased out in the same way as the MCA and that in the meantime it be converted into an extended zero rate band as described above for the MCA.

The tax treatment of families with children

Child tax allowances were abolished in 1979 following the decision by the Labour Government to combine child tax allowances and family allowances into a single tax-free cash benefit (child benefit). In this way the help given to families with children was made independent of the level of income (whereas child tax allowances were worth more to those with higher incomes). It is also an important feature of child benefit that it is paid to the mother.

Child benefit has not been popular with the Conservative Government and its real value has been eroded. A number of commentators (including Frank Field MP) have argued that child benefit would be less subject to Conservative hostility if it were made once again a child tax allowance. There does indeed seem merit in designing Labour policy so that it stands more chance of surviving a Conservative onslaught. This does not however lead us to support the idea of the re-introduction of child tax allowances. These would mean, particularly with the graduated structure of rates, that the better-off families would derive disproportionate benefit.

We also considered the possibility that child benefit be payable as a tax credit. A refundable tax credit is different from a tax allowance in that it is worth the same flat rate to everyone, regardless of whether they are taxpayers or their marginal tax rate. Before the introduction of independent taxation it was not possible to convert child benefit into a child credit and keep the mother as the recipient in all cases, but under this proposal, the full, flat-rate value of the payment is unconditionally hers. This change would not affect the recipients in any very material way, but it would mean that child tax credits were treated in government accounting as a deduction from taxes rather than as an addition to spending. A government which raised child tax credits could claim to be cutting taxes. Such a change would however be purely cosmetic.

Another frequent proposal is that child benefit should be taxed. There are arguments both for and against. With a graduated rate structure the arguments for taxing benefits as a means of targetting may well be stronger, and we suggest that the issue be looked at again when the graduated rate structure is in place. A more immediate priority is to raise the level of child benefit.

There can be little doubt that an effective solution to the problem of the poverty trap requires a sizeable increase in child benefit, designed to float families off dependence on family credit, and we see this as an essential part of Labour's policy. In our view, alternative suggestions of a benefit credit, withdrawn with income and related devices, can only reduce the severity of the poverty trap for some families at the expense of raising marginal tax rates to an unacceptable level for other families. And it is possible to improve the targetting of child benefit by making it age-related and paying a higher rate of benefit for the first child.

Age allowance

For people aged 65 and over there is a higher personal allowance, the age allowance. This means that a single person aged between 65 and 74 has an allowance of £3,400 in place of £2,785, and for a single person aged 75 or over the allowance is £3,540. This benefits elderly taxpayers and those who would otherwise be liable for tax by a maximum of £2.95 (aged 65 to 74) or £3.63 (aged 75 or over) a week. The benefit is withdrawn

Chart 6.1: Income tax schedule for the over-65s in 1989/90

Single person aged under 75

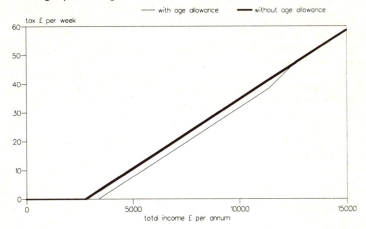

from those with income in excess of £11,400 at the rate of £1 of allowance for every £2 of income until it is extinguished.

When looked at closely, the age allowance appears rather strange. Chart 6.1 shows the 1989/90 income tax schedule for a single person aged 70, both with and without the age allowance. (The corresponding diagrams for married men or for those aged over 75 are similar.) Its effect is to benefit those pensioners with incomes in excess of the tax threshold excluding the best-off (about the top 10 per cent) of the elderly. It provides no benefit at all to the bottom *half* of pensioners whose incomes place them below the income tax threshold. This pattern does not appear to us to be justified on distributional grounds. It would be better for the money to be redirected to an increase in social security benefits for the elderly.

The post-1990 system will retain the age allowance and will allow husband and wife to receive a married couple's age allowance according to the age of the elder spouse (£1,985 if aged 65-74, £2,025 if aged 75 or over), while each partner will receive a single age allowance in their own right. This means that some pensioner couples will gain: if they are both over 65 and both receive age allowance under the new system. Under the old system the maximum allowance they could jointly receive would be the married man's age allowance plus the standard wife's earned income allowance (£5,385 + £2,785 = £8,170 per year for a couple aged under 75). Under the new system the maximum would be two single age allowances plus a married couple's age allowance (2 x £3,400 + £1,985 = £8,785). In addition, the income limit for age allowance is to be applied at the same rate as currently for the couple's income, but separately for each spouse. In some circumstances this will extend the range of joint income over which the higher age allowances apply. There are also some cases where there may be a loss: for example, husbands aged under 65 with wives aged over 65 who lose the advantage that the wife could claim the full married age allowance including the single element for her husband. There are transitional protection provisions to cover this group.

The main justification for the age allowance and its retention in the new system seems to be the administrative saving from keeping out of the tax net pensioners with little other income besides the state pension. We can see the merit in this argument, but suggest that it may also be met by a general increase in the tax threshold. As we have proposed in Chapter 5, the threshold should be significantly increased.

We therefore recommend that the basic National Insurance pension be increased and that the age allowance be abolished. In order to compensate for the loss of age allowance (at a tax rate of 25 per cent in 1989/90) the National Insurance pension would have to be increased by £3 a week for a single person and £4.85 for a couple, with an addition of £0.60 for single pensioners aged 75 or over and £0.90 for couples over that age. Since this would raise the incomes of all pensioners, except for those on income support, and not just those currently benefitting from the age allowance, it would have a net cost in excess of the saving on the age allowance of some £900 million. The rise in basic state pension is however part of Labour's programme and in this sense our recommendation may be seen as one method of financing the increased spending. In effect, it is an element of base broadening, an approach considered further in the next chapter.

Conclusions

The basic principle of taxation for husbands and wives should be that of independence, with fully separate taxation and full privacy in tax affairs. The Committee recommends that the single person's allowance be significantly increased and the married couple's allowance reduced at the same time. This policy would allow the married couple's allowance to be phased out with no reduction in the amount of tax-free income received by any married couple, and with an increase for many couples. The rise in the single person's allowance would also allow the additional personal allowance to be phased out for single parents. As far as families with children are concerned, the Committee would give priority to a sizeable increase in child benefit. A substantial increase in the National Insurance pension should be the occasion for the abolition of the age allowance.

Chapter 7

Broadening the income tax base

The basis for personal taxation that we are recommending is that of a comprehensive income tax, with departures from that "ideal" justified by reasons of principle or practice. In our concrete proposals we are seeking to broaden the tax base, reversing the erosion that has taken place as successive governments have "charged more and more on less and less". We believe that the strategy of charging a lower rate of tax on a broader tax base is one of the keys to successful tax reform in Britain, allowing Labour to finance its spending programme while reducing rates of taxation. There are also good distributional grounds for base broadening, in that the *average* taxpayer derives little benefit from many of the concessions which have eroded the tax base.

In this chapter we consider in more detail the application of this approach, considering both the treatment of particular sources of income and more general issues such as the taxation of real versus money income from investment and the introduction of a maximum allowance. Our discussion refers at a number of points to the taxation of capital gains but this subject is treated more fully in Chapter 9.

One of the principal aims of a broader tax base is to allow tax rates to be reduced. For this reason the size of existing tax concessions is important background information. In Table 7.1 we list the official Inland Revenue estimates of the cost of some of the major tax reliefs and exemptions (the list is not exhaustive). The extent to which they accurately measure the cost of departures from a comprehensive income tax base is discussed below when we come to individual items.

In considering the size of the amounts in Table 7.1, it should be borne in mind that a 1p increase in the basic rate of income tax in 1988/9 would have raised some £1,250 million in revenue. If revenue could be increased by £13,410 million — which is the sum of the items in the table — then on the face of it the basic rate could be cut by about 10p in the £. Such a calculation is not of course valid as it stands. To begin with, the "cost" of the tax reliefs depend on the tax rate itself and would be smaller with a basic rate of 15 per cent.

Secondly, it takes no account of changes consequent on the removal of tax relief. One obvious example is that if National Savings ceased to be tax-exempt then the government would probably have to pay a higher gross rate of interest in order to attract funds. The net saving to the Treasury would be less than indicated. Working in the opposite direction is the fact that the total impact of abolishing reliefs is greater than the sum of the items in Table 7.1, since the removal of one tax exemption or relief may bring additional taxpayers into the tax net or move them into the higher rate band. To the extent that is possible, we take account of these considerations in our later analysis. For the present, however, the figures in Table 7.1 certainly suggest that there is scope for significant rate reductions through broadening of the income tax base.

Table 7.1 Inland Revenue estimates of cost of tax reliefs and exemptions

	£ million in 1988/9
Mortgage interest relief	5,500
Social security benefits	850
of which:	
NI sickness, invalidity benefit	370
Supplementary benefit/FIS	140*
War widows and disability	105
Industrial disablement	70
Attendance and mobility allowances	130
Private pensions:	
Investment income of occupational pension schemes	4,400
Lump sum payments to occupational pensioners	1,000
Contributions to personal pensions	425
Life assurance premium relief	480
Other savings:	
Exemption of National Savings interest	390+
Business Expansion Scheme	100+
Personal Equity Plans	15+
Profit-sharing and share option schemes	50+

* Figure is for 1987/88
+ Figures subject to a wide margin of error.

The reader may suspect that, if the tax base could be broadened easily, then the Chancellor of the Exchequer would have found it attractive to do so before now. The reason that he has not done so reflects the fact that base-broadening is not costless — both because there are those who would be losers (the loss of the tax exemption outweighing for them the advantage of lower tax rates) and because the exemptions contribute to other policy objectives. The classic example is that of mortgage interest relief and it is with this that we begin.

Mortgage interest relief and the taxation of owner-occupiers

Mortgage interest is currently allowed against taxable income on mortgages up to £30,000 per dwelling, so that with interest rates of 14.5 per cent there is a maximum saving in tax of £1,088 a year for a basic rate taxpayer and £1,740 for a higher rate taxpayer. The basic rate relief is provided at source (hence the name MIRAS for Mortgage Interest Relief At Source), which means that non-taxpayers also derive the benefit at the basic rate. This tax relief is in effect a subsidy to borrowing for house purchase and its cost has grown with the expansion of owner-occupation. In 1979/80 the estimated cost was £1.45 billion, compared with £5.5 billion in 1988/9 in Table 7.1. At the same time, the size of the subsidy depends on the tax rate: compared to the time when the basic rate was 33 per cent, the government is now subsidising a quarter of the mortgage interest payment rather than nearly a third. In the case of non-taxpayers, they actually *lose* overall when the basic rate is reduced, since they have to pay more for their mortgages. With a £30,000 mortgage, they would see their payments rise by £3.75 per week if the basic rate were reduced from 25 per cent to 20 per cent.

While this MIRAS relief is the item included in Table 7.1, it does not represent a proper measure of the tax advantage enjoyed by owner-occupiers under the UK income tax. Indeed it might well appear strange to an outsider that there should be any question of *not* allowing interest paid as a deductible expense, just as interest *received* is a taxable item. If a person borrowed £100,000 at an interest rate of 10 per cent to buy machinery which generated £15,000 income, then the net income would be £15,000 less the interest cost of £10,000. If the £100,000 were borrowed to buy a house, then it might seem natural that the interest remained equally deductible. The problem is however that — for owner-occupied houses — no counterpart of the income enters the tax base. If the house were let, then there would be rent, but if the owner occupies the house then no cash changes hands.

The fact that no cash changes hands does not prevent the income from owner-occupied housing being treated as taxable income. Under the old Schedule A of the income tax, a notional income was attributed to owner-occupiers based in principle on the amount of rent that could have been obtained. The fact that these "deemed consumption benefits", as they are termed by the CBI, that owner-occupiers can be assumed to derive from living in their own houses are not included in the tax base represents a departure from the comprehensive definition of income (the same applies to the failure to include capital gains on owner-occupied houses, a point to which we return in Chapter 9). The same could be said about other assets owned by households, such as consumer durables, cars, yachts and pictures. In quantitative terms, however, it is owner-occupied housing which is the most significant. While the calculation of use value or "imputed rent" is surrounded by problems, by any measure the figure is likely to be high. According to the rather conservative estimates of the Central Statistical Office, for example, the total imputed rent of owner-occupiers in 1987 was £14.6 billion (*United Kingdom National Accounts 1988 Edition*, Table 4.1). If this were taxed at 25 per cent, then the addition to total revenue would be £3,650 million.

It would be possible to re-introduce the taxation of the imputed rent on owner-occupied houses, based for example on the capital value of the property, in which case there would be no case for removing the relief for mortgage interest and indeed there would be no justification for the £30,000 limit. Or this would be the case for the *real* element of the interest (the issue of real or money interest was discussed in Chapter 4). The effects of the introduction of a capital value charge on owner-occupiers, coupled with abolition of the £30,000 limit, would be to shift the burden of taxation towards those who have already paid off their mortgages and away from those with large mortgages. It would tend to benefit the young at the expense of the middle-aged and elderly. In the latter case there may well be problems of liquidity, in that the income tax payments on imputed rent would have to met out of current cash income.

The principal argument against such a re-introduction of the tax on imputed rent is that owner-occupation is an activity which the Labour Party would not want to discourage. The exemption of imputed rent provides a *general* subsidy, although it is one that rises with the marginal tax rate and hence provides greater benefit to higher rate taxpayers (a fact that would become more important with our proposed graduated structure). It does not seem to us the best approach; we would prefer to see the subsidy explicitly treated as such and of equal value to all owner-occupiers, whether taxpayers or not. In the past, the advantage that housing has enjoyed has in part been offset by local authority rates. Their abolition leaves a hole in the tax system which we discuss further in Chapter 11. We do however accept that the taxation of imputed rent under the income tax is not likely to be politically feasible. It would certainly be open to mis-representation by Labour's opponents.

Accepting that the imputed rent from owner-occupation cannot be included in the tax base, we are left with the question of mortgage interest relief. The answer given here by the Conservatives is clear but little advertised. With the exception of the increase from £25,000 to £30,000 in 1983/4, the Conservatives have left this relief to be eroded by inflation. This is shown clearly in Chart 7.1. In 1979, the ceiling represented some 125 per cent of the price of an average house bought through a building society; in 1988 it represented some 61 per cent. But since the early 1980s, lenders other than building societies have provided a substantial share of the larger mortgages, so if all mortgages were included, the current figure would probably' be smaller still. Assuming the costs of a first-time buyer continue to rise at the same rate as they have over the last 10 years, by the end of the century the relief will represent only 31 per cent of a new 100 per cent mortgage. (A further erosion has been the restriction of the £30,000 limit to one dwelling, preventing unmarried couples and groups of single people from claiming more than one relief per dwelling.)

Chart 7.1: Mortgage interest tax relief ceiling
As a % of average house prices 1979-88

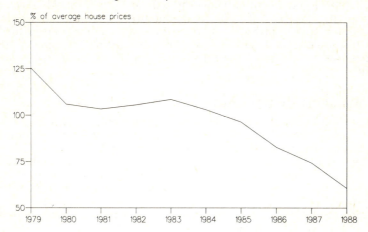

Given that there are other fiscal advantages to owner-occupation (including the fact that imputed rent is not taxed and the exemption of capital gains), our view is that the Conservatives have been right in deciding that the relief should be progressively withdrawn. If it is desired to help first-time buyers, and those at the stage of the life-cycle when pressure is particularly great, then this is better achieved by explicit, targetted subsidies. What is needed is a more flexible policy that aims to produce more housing rather than piecemeal measures that push up the price of existing housing. Tax policy alone cannot achieve this and a coherent and comprehensive housing strategy is also required. We recommend that the £30,000 limit not be increased with inflation. This is consistent with official Labour policy that mortgage interest relief should continue to be paid, but would mean that the cost of this tax expenditure would be progressively reduced. The redistribution of the tax burden would be achieved gradually, without the immediate cash losers that there would be if MIRAS were abolished overnight.

Turning to the rate at which relief would be allowed, there is, in our view, no reason why relief should be allowed at higher rates of tax. The logic of the way in which MIRAS is administered is such that relief at a single rate would be simpler and it would mean the same proportional subsidy (up to the ceiling) for all. There remains the question of the choice of rate. The Policy Review in its Final Report stated that this would be "equivalent to the basic rate relief which we inherit" (*Meet the Challenge, Make the Change*, page 73). This would amount to relief of 25 per cent in 1989/90. This is one possible option; a second is that the relief be set at the *initial* rate of tax in a graduated structure. In both cases, we see merit in the proposal that the relief be redesignated as an explicit interest rate subsidy and accounted for as public expenditure: for example a 3 per cent subsidy (up to the ceiling) rather than relief of 25 per cent on interest of 12 per cent. Moreover, this could subsequently be taken further to provide a more flexible pattern of relief over time. A system of credits could be devised which concentrated subsidy on those in most need — such as first time buyers, or those at particular stages of the lifecycle.

Social security benefits

The present tax treatment of social security benefits lacks any apparent rationale. In principle, all such benefits should be included according to the comprehensive definition of the tax base, and we have to ask why certain benefits are at present exempt from taxation. As indicated in Table 7.1, the revenue foregone is estimated at some £850 million. In considering the treatment of individual benefits, it is helpful to take separately:

(a) means-tested benefits, such as income support (previously supplementary benefit), which are designed to bring incomes up to a specified minimum level or which restrict entitlement to those below a specified ceiling;

(b) benefits such as child benefit and those for the disabled which compensate for their higher costs of everyday life;

(c) National Insurance (NI) and other benefits which are paid in replacement of earnings and which are not subject to a means-test.

There is an element of circularity in the taxation of benefits. If everyone paid tax at a rate of 25 per cent, then a benefit of £7.50 free of tax would be equivalent in terms of cash income to a taxable benefit of £10, but in the latter case the government would be paying out more and then collecting it back in again. This may suggest that all benefits should be tax-free. However, people do not all pay the same marginal rates of tax. Even with the present structure, there are non-taxpayers who would — in this example — receive the full £10, and there are higher rate taxpayers whose net benefit would be limited to £6. This would become even more important with a graduated rate structure of the kind proposed in Chapter 5. Taking an illustrative "four rate" structure (20, 36, 41 and 50 per cent), a £5 a week increase in the retirement pension would mean £5 extra to the non-taxpaying pensioner, £4 to those in the first band of taxable income, £3.20 to those in the next, £2.95 to those in the next and £2.50 to the best-off. In this way, the gain would be tailored to income without need for a means-test.

There is however one case in which the circularity does not seem justified: in the case of means-tested benefits such as income support, Family Credit, housing benefit, educational maintenance allowances, hospital patients' travelling expenses, and uniform and clothing grants. Means-tested benefits are in effect a parallel system of taxation, with benefits based on assessed income; and, as presently designed, this assessment is based on income net of income tax (and NIC). To make these benefits taxable in turn would serve no evident purpose and it would add to the already great administrative burdens on individual claimants and government officials. (It is of course an important aim of Labour policy to reduce dependence on means-tested benefits.) In view of these considerations we accept the present situation whereby means-tested benefits remain tax-free. There is however at present an exception to this rule. Income support for the unemployed and those involved in trade disputes was made taxable by the Conservatives in 1982. In our view there are no grounds for distinguishing between these and other groups of recipients, and we recommend that all income support payments be tax-free. This would be an administrative simplification.

A second case where we may not wish to tax social security benefits concerns those benefits which make provision for additional costs of living of families in different circumstances. This is the case at present with child benefit and there may be other contingencies for which similar provision should be made, an obvious example being the costs of disability: ie we may not wish to tax social security benefits which seek to compensate for the higher living costs of the disabled (group (b) above). In such a case we would be using the assessment of disability for benefit purposes as a means of identifying those to whom preferential treatment should be given also under the tax system. In the system of disability benefits that applies at the time of writing, this applies to attendance allowance, mobility allowance, and to the constant attendance allowance and exceptionally severe disablement allowance paid with industrial disablement benefit. These are at present tax-free, and we recommend that this continue. (There is case for converting the tax exemption into a tax credit, so as not to give larger benefit to higher rate taxpayers, but we do not feel that the administrative cost in this case would be warranted.)

The third category (c) consists of benefits paid in replacement of earnings which are not means-tested. This includes NI retirement pensions, NI widows' benefits and NI unemployment benefit, all of which are subject to income tax. The logic of taxing such benefits is illustrated by statutory sick pay, which is in effect a continuation of payment by the employer during short-term sickness: if the gross payment were the same but not taxable, then the employee would be better off when sick. By the same logic, however, the short-term NI sickness benefit (for those not covered by statutory sick pay) should be taxable. At present it is not taxable, not having been brought into the tax net at the same time as NI unemployment benefit in July 1982, and we recommend that it become taxable. The same applies to the NI maternity allowance (payable to those not covered by statutory maternity pay), which should also in our view be made taxable.

The changes proposed in the previous paragraph would bring all short-term NI benefits into tax. But there are other NI benefits which serve the function of income replacement which are at present tax-free and which should in our view be brought into tax. This applies to NI invalidity benefit, payable to those who have been off work for more than 28 weeks, which may include an earnings-related additional pension as under SERPS. The fact that this is tax-free, whereas the retirement pension is taxable, means that it may be to the advantage of the elderly to postpone retirement and to continue to receive invalidity benefit as long as permitted. In our view, invalidity pensions, invalidity allowance and the severe disablement allowance should be brought into taxation. In the same way we recommend that the reduced earnings allowance payable in cases of industrial disability and the industrial disablement pension become subject to tax. In the cases where these benefits continue to include additions for dependent children, these additions should not be taxed, as is the case with the NI pension additions at the moment. The same argument could be applied in favour of taxing certain war disablement benefits and war widows' pensions, but — whatever the logic — no Chancellor of the Exchequer is likely to take the step of taxing war pensions. We accept that in this case there are over-riding considerations and do not recommend that war pensions be taxable.

The proposals made above would rationalise the present tax treatment of social security benefits so that means-tested benefits and certain benefits designed to meet the higher living costs of the disabled would be tax-free, but that benefits designed to replace earnings should be taxable (with the exception of war pensions). These changes — with the exception of that concerning the unemployed and those in industrial disputes — would reduce, other things being equal, the net incomes of social security recipients. However, providing that the tax-free band of income were set at an appropriate level — and the proposal in Chapter 5 was to significantly increase this band for most people — tax would only be paid by those with significant additional income. Only people who were on short-term benefits — and quickly returned to higher incomes — or those who received substantial incomes from other sources would actually pay any tax on their benefits. Furthermore, other things would not be equal under a Labour Government, which has already made clear that the improvement of social security is a major priority. The changes proposed in the tax treatment of social security should therefore be seen as part of a package of measures where there would be significant increases in such benefits, as with those for the disabled.

Occupational pensions and retirement relief

In addition to state pensions, people make provision for retirement through occupational pension schemes, through personal pensions and through personal saving. In the case of employees, membership in an approved occupational scheme, or an appropriate personal pension scheme, allows them to contract out of the state earnings related scheme. This occupational or personal pension provision enjoys favourable tax treatment. In the case of occupational schemes which are approved by the Inland Revenue:
- employee contributions are tax-deductible for income tax purposes;
- employer contributions may be set against corporation tax and they are not regarded as a benefit in kind to employees;

- income and capital gains accruing to the pension fund are free of tax;
- pensions received are taxed under income tax, but part of the pension may be paid as a tax-free lump sum on retirement.

There is a maximum to the total pension which can be provided under a tax-approved scheme, which for new entrants from June 1989 is two-thirds of £60,000; the 1989 Budget also introduced a ceiling to the total tax relief for new entrants from June 1989 which limits the relevant earnings to £60,000. In the case of approved personal pensions, the provisions are similar, subject to a limit on the contributions which can be paid, rising from 17.5 per cent of earnings at age 35 or less to 35 per cent at age 56 and over. (Personal pensions replaced, in the case of the self-employed, the earlier provisions for retirement annuity relief.)

Private pensions are often described as "tax exempt". The extent to which this is true may be seen by a comparison with the case where a person saves £75 out of post-tax income, which at a rate of 25 per cent is equivalent to £100 pre-tax, and invests this in an asset which yields a tax-free return (say owner-occupied housing or, since 1988, forestry). The accumulated return plus original capital is, say £150 when withdrawing and this is by assumption tax-free. In the case of an occupational pension, the contributions are in fact allowed out of *pre-tax* income, so that the person can save £100, leading to a total withdrawal on retirement of £200, but the pension is taxable, so that this is reduced to £150. So that, by levying a tax on an "exit" basis, we are treating the occupational pension in the same way as a tax-free investment. When people complain about being taxed on their pensions, they should remember that the income which they contributed was tax-free at the outset.

But there are two important respects in which the income tax treatment of occupational pensions is in fact more favourable than tax exemption. First, the fact that the tax is paid on an "exit" basis means that the rate of tax actually paid is likely to be lower than that which would have been paid at the time of the contributions. It allows the well-paid employee to transfer income from a time when he or she is earning enough to pay a rate of 40 per cent to retirement when the rate is more likely to be 25 per cent. With the graduated rate structure this benefit will be potentially greater; however, we do not believe that it would be feasible for this advantage to be eliminated. If employee contributions were made taxable, then there would be a switch to employer contributions, with schemes becoming non-contributory. There would be considerable transitional problems, lasting for up to half a century, since taxes would continue to be levied on an "exit" basis on pensions where the contributions had been tax-free. We recommend therefore that contributions to occupational pension schemes should continue to be tax-deductible.

The second advantage to occupational pensions is the provision which allows part of a person's pension rights to be paid out as a tax-free lump sum. Successive official inquiries have concluded that this practice has no justification: for example the Royal Commission on the Taxation of Profits and Income (*Final Report*, 1955, page 23). The present Government has recognised that this concession is open to question. An upper limit of £150,000 has been imposed on new entrants to schemes after March 1987, and the new provisions in the 1989 Budget mean that the maximum lump-sum for occupational pensions is reduced to £90,000 for new entrants. (There is no corresponding maximum figure for personal pensions.)

We can see no justification for lump-sums being tax-free, other than the expectations which have been formed as a result of its existence. We recommend that the process set in train by the Conservative Government should be taken further, with the £90,000 limit applied to all pensions, not just new entrants. In this way the effect on decisions about early retirement is likely to be minimal. One of the effects of imposing a limit only on new entrants, as at present, is to lock top managers into their current employment. Extending the limit to pensions already accruing will remove this lock-in effect. Very few people would see the lump sum they expect to receive affected in any way. Even in the public sector where taking some part of the pension as a lump sum is obligatory and popular, it would be a long time before the £90,000 limit had any widespread effect. For example, the maximum possible lump sum that could be received by a head teacher retiring in 1990 at the top of the salary scale after the maximum number of years service is about £51,000.

There remains the important question of whether the income of the funds accumulated by occupational and personal pension schemes should continue to have tax-free status (which would not be changed by the proposals made above). One major argument is that saving for retirement is an activity which the government wishes to encourage, like owner-occupation. People may not, unaided, make sufficient provision for their old age, and to the extent that they fail to do so, then the cost falls on a future government which has to provide income support. We find some merit in this argument, but we are not convinced that it justifies the full exemption of pension fund income, particularly when it is borne in mind that pensions would still have the favoured "exit" treatment (see above).

The approach we favour is that the social security tax on investment income proposed in Chapter 8 be levied also on pension fund income and capital gains. It would then apply to the pension fund business of life assurance companies as well as self-administered schemes.

It can be argued that the consequences of the introduction of a tax on the investment income of pension funds may include an increase in contributions, a reduction in benefits paid, a reduction in reserves, changes in the pattern of investment, and changes in the form of organisation of pension schemes. Such reactions have in turn implications for individual taxpayers and for the government. If, for example, employees have to contribute more, then this has a direct effect on their net incomes not different in kind from that which would result if the contributions ceased to be tax-deductible. The increased employee contributions would also attract further relief. If employer contributions were increased, then this might be passed on in prices or lead to a downward pressure on wages; it would certainly reduce the government's revenue from corporation tax. It is however the Committee's view that a tax at a relatively low rate may well be accommodated, in that some schemes may at present be over-funded, and there will not necessarily be reactions of the kind described above. It also seems unlikely that a tax of 9 per cent would be sufficient to induce schemes to change their legal structure; it is however the case that investment policy is likely to be changed, with funds switching out of gilts, and that this may raise the cost to the government of financing its borrowing.

Life assurance and private medical insurance

Conservative policy with regard to these two forms of insurance has moved in totally different directions. In the case of life assurance, relief used to be given for premiums paid for qualifying policies at a rate equal to half the basic rate of tax. In 1984 Mr Lawson abolished this relief for new contracts of life assurance, so that although the cost is still quite substantial (see Table 7.1) it is declining over time. This was a significant step towards broadening the tax base. The only modification that we propose, in line with the reductions which have been made in the relief as the basic rate has been cut, is that the rate of relief be set at half the initial rate of tax with the graduated structure.

The government has moved in the opposite direction with regard to medical insurance. The introduction from April 1990 of tax relief for premiums paid for private medical insurance on behalf of people aged over 60 is a narrowing of the tax base, with an estimated cost of £40 million. In the context of Labour's planned National Health Initiative we can see no justification for this relief under a Labour government and propose its abolition.

We have also considered the taxation of the life assurance industry, which has long been felt to be unsatisfactory. The consultative document put out by the Inland Revenue in 1988 said that the current tax regime for life assurance

> "does not perform well. First, and crucially, it does not produce a tax yield commensurate with the profits earned by offices and the income and gains earned for, and paid out to, policy holders. This shortfall in yield does not reflect any specific decision to provide special tax privileges for life assurance"
> (The Taxation of Life Assurance, 1988, para 13.2).

As an example of the yield shortfall, the Revenue calculated that if the non-pension life business had been treated in the same way as an authorised unit trust then the yield would have been between two and three times greater than it actually was (1988, para 6.9). The difference in 1986 would have been some £700-800 million even at the basic rate of tax.

Following a review of this problem, the Chancellor announced in his 1989 Budget a number of changes along the line of reforming the current rules rather than introducing a new tax regime. These include:
i) the separation of pension and non-pension business, so that the expenses of the former cannot be used to reduce the tax base of the latter

(introduction of a "ring-fence");

(ii) allowing expenses of acquiring new life business as a deduction spread over 7 years rather than immediate deduction as at present;

(iii) reduction in the tax rate on income and gains attributable to policy holders from 35 per cent and 30 per cent respectively to 25 per cent;

(iv) abolition of the life assurance policy duty.

Certain of these changes, such as the ring-fence, are, in our view, steps in the right direction, but they do not go sufficiently far in increasing the tax paid by the life assurance industry. This is demonstrated by the fact that the long-term yield is expected to be only £250 million a year (*Financial Statement and Budget Report 1989-90*, pages 53-4), which is only about a third of the figure quoted above for 1986.

In our view the relief for life assurance initial costs should be abolished altogether, a move which is described by the Revenue as "more consistent than the current rules with the treatment of other forms of personal investment" (1988, para 10.23). To the extent that it errs in the opposite direction, we would argue that it is a *quid pro quo* for the abolition of life assurance policy duty and that the discouragement to spending on marketing costs would be welcome (and impose no loss on the policy holders). We also believe that the corporation tax treatment of life assurance profits needs to be examined more closely. Finally, we see merit in the introduction of a minimum tax provision, to ensure that the tax yield from life assurance does not fall below some specified proportion of that applicable under other regimes such as that for unit trusts.

Composite rate tax

Before turning to tax incentives for the wealthy, we should draw attention to the tax penalty imposed on small savers through the composite rate of tax (CRT). Under CRT a fixed rate of tax (currently 21.75 per cent) is charged on interest paid by a range of institutions, and while this is grossed up for higher rate taxpayers, with the tax paid treated as 25 per cent, non-taxpayers are unable to recoup the tax paid.

The rate of CRT is calculated as an *average* of the tax that would be due from those liable at the basic rate (including the basic rate part of higher rate tax) and from non-taxpayers. This means that taxpayers benefit and non-taxpayers lose. The scope of CRT has been extended by the present Government so as to include bank interest, and calculations for 1987/88 suggest that £450 million is collected from those who are not taxpayers (*Hansard* vol 147, 1989 col 84). The principal reason for this system is administrative simplicity, and we do not believe that this justifies the evident inequity. We therefore propose the abolition of composite rate tax and its replacement by a withholding tax. This would mean higher rate taxpayers would be credited only with this amount of tax and additional higher rates would be paid, and that non-taxpayers could claim repayment. (The administrative aspects are discussed in Chapter 12.)

Savings incentives for the wealthy

Erosion of the tax base under the Conservatives has been particularly noticeable in the area of savings incentives such as the Business Expansion Scheme (BES) and Personal Equity Plans (PEPs). There has been a whole series of schemes introduced with the ostensible purpose of encouraging savings. The main effect of these schemes has been to allow a small number of people to avoid tax, while they have proved an inefficient way of raising savings and promoting enterprise. The total cost (Table 7.1) may be smaller than for some other items, but the nature of the schemes is such that the advantage has been heavily concentrated on those at the top of the income distribution. In addition there are long-standing concessions such as those on National Savings.

The BES offers full income tax relief on up to £40,000 a year invested in new equity of unquoted UK companies, carrying on a trade or letting residential property, which must be held for 5 years. Capital gains tax is then not payable when the shares are first sold. This is a clear example of the government using the fiscal system to intervene in the allocation of resources (as with the extension in 1988 to include residential property for letting) and we consider this form of incentive to invest to be mis-directed and unduly expensive. We therefore propose that the BES be abolished with immediate effect, so that no new investments may be made in this form. This means that tax exemptions of inflows of savings into BES would be ended at once.

Personal Equity Plans allow people to hold their savings in a form where the income is tax-free (both income and capital gains), as with owner-occupied houses. A taxpayer may invest up to £4,800 a year in a registered PEP, which has to be substantially invested in UK shares. Introduced in 1987 the amount of revenue foregone is so far small, but it will build up steadily (in contrast to the BES where the tax relief is provided at the outset, the saving arises when the income is received). Again we do not agree that this tax exemption serves a useful purpose and we recommend that PEPs should be abolished, with the income and gains becoming taxable.

National Savings are not a form of savings associated particularly with the wealthy; it is however the higher rate taxpayers who derive most benefit from these concessions. It is no accident that the first 6 sections of Tolley's *Tax Efficient Personal Investments* (1986) deal with National Savings and Premium Bonds. Not only is the first £70 of interest credited to a National Savings Bank ordinary account free of income and capital gains tax but National Savings certificates offer a "government investment of particular value to the higher rate taxpayer" (*Tolley's*, 1986, page 4). This is because the yield that the government has to offer to be competitive with taxable forms of investment depends on the tax rate of the average investor. A basic rate taxpayer would be indifferent between 10 per cent in an account taxed at 25 per cent and a tax-free National Savings investment at 7.5 per cent, but the higher-rate taxpayer would do better with the latter. There are limits to the amounts that can be invested in National Savings but they are quite generous (£10,000 for some schemes plus a limit of £200 invested per month for others), and allow a substantial level of income to be received tax-free if all opportunities are utilised.

We do not consider that it would be appropriate to apply withholding tax to National Savings for two reasons. The first is the administrative problem of repaying small amounts of interest to holders of accounts in the National Savings Bank. The second is that future Chancellors may wish, for conjunctural reasons, to stimulate savings, and the attractions of issuing tax-free National Savings certificates may well prove irresistible.

Work expenses

Work expenses are not included in Table 7.1 because they are an item which should in principle be deducted from gross income to arrive at the net income from employment. In our view such expenses should in principle be deductible, but they should be tightly defined. For this purpose we accept the current principle under which expenses are defined under Schedule E. Work expenses are currently allowed against tax to a very limited extent for ordinary employees (under Schedule E of the income tax). The expenses must be "wholly, exclusively and necessarily" (or "necessarily" in the case of travelling expenses) incurred "in the performance of duties". For example, expenses incurred prior to entering into duties (eg travel to work) or in preparation for them (eg taking driving lessons) are not allowed against tax since they fail the test of being incurred in the performance of duties. The areas for which employees can claim work expenses include tools, special clothing etc not provided by the employer. These are mostly agreed with the relevant trade unions, the rates in 1988 including £40 for uniformed police officers, £50 for agricultural workers, and £80 for carpenters, cabinet makers, joiners, wood carvers and woodcutting machinists. They include subscriptions to professional associations and bodies "for advancing and spreading knowledge". The total cost is estimated to be £320 million in 1986/7. The more generous treatment of expenses under Schedule D and its possible abuses are discussed in Chapter 10.

One particular class of expenses which is not covered by the Schedule E definition is that of childcare costs. Whether childcare costs should be allowed as a tax deduction — or generate a tax credit — generates strong arguments on either side. On the one hand, the experience of working parents who see childcare costs as unavoidable in allowing them to take paid employment suggests that they should be tax-deductible. Many such parents would regard their net income from work as being after deduction of childcare costs. If income after this deduction is used to determine comparability, the fact that childcare costs are not tax deductible violates horizontal equity, as those with children are being more heavily taxed than those without. The lack of deductibility also means that the net return from a second partner taking paid employment can be very small, acting as a disincentive to labour force participation. Giving a tax credit or deduction would also provide support to more flexible forms of childcare than can be provided through directly subsidised local authority nurseries or those provided by employers.

On the other hand, there are also strong arguments against such a change. In particular, supporting childcare through the tax system could generate vertical inequities. Relief could be given as a credit, to be of equal value to all taxpayers whatever their marginal rate, and could be subject to a limit so as to put a cap on the gain to those employing the most expensive nannies. Even so, it would still only benefit taxpayers, giving no help to those on the lowest incomes who would need it most. Although this kind of argument can be put against virtually any adjustment to improve horizontal equity between taxpayers, it does have force in this case given the very large loss of revenue which could be involved. If resources for assisting with childcare are limited, channelling them through the tax system is not very progressive compared with the alternatives of, say, increasing child benefit for all pre-school children or giving direct subsidy to forms of provision which will be used by non-taxpayers as well as taxpayers. If the problem that is being addressed is the extra cost — either actual or through foregone income — borne by those with pre-school age children, it is more logical to help with that cost for everyone affected than to try to work through the tax system. This is, after all, analogous to the arguments for child benefit rather than child tax allowances or for the National Health Service rather than tax deductible private health insurance.

There is, however, one way in which we are persuaded that the tax system should be adjusted. We recommend that employer-subsidised nurseries for children should not be a chargeable benefit for tax purposes where they are generally available to all employees. We hope that this will serve to encourage employers to make such provision and that other initiatives, apart from through the tax system, will be taken to encourage the expansion of the full range of quality childcare services.

Fringe benefits and share options

Remuneration paid to employees in the form of fringe benefits is as much part of the comprehensive tax base as remuneration paid in the form of wages or salaries. This has been accepted by successive Chancellors who have sought to bring benefits in kind within the scope of income taxation, particularly through the extended provisions for directors and employees earning more than a specified limit (which has been £8,500 a year, including the benefits, since 1979/80).

Our basic principle is that, as far as is administratively feasible, for reasons of fairness, benefits in kind should be subject to the full rates of income tax. We did examine the idea of a separate tax on fringe benefits along the lines introduced by the Labor Government in Australia in 1986, but concluded that the circumstances were sufficiently different that the same arguments did not apply. In the Australian case, there had been no systematic taxation of fringe benefits prior to that date, whereas previous Labour, and indeed Conservative, Chancellors have brought important items such as company cars into the scope of taxation. The approach which we recommend is therefore that of strengthening the existing income tax provisions. This would include the gradual extension of these provisions to all employees through continuing the Conservative policy of maintaining the £8,500 limit unchanged in money terms.

For individual items of benefits in kind there are adjustments which should be made. We have referred above to the taxation of the benefit deriving from the provision of employer-subsidised nurseries and recommended its abolition. In the case of company cars, Mr Lawson in his 1988 Budget doubled the scale charge, and in 1989 increased it by a further third. They do however need to be kept under review and we recommend that a formula be established to provide automatic adjustment with changing prices and interest rates. Moreover, there is a case for more steps in the scale and extending the scale so as to increase the taxation on the most expensive cars. More widely, the issue should be seen in the context of Labour's transport policy.

The most important change with respect to benefits in kind is, in our view, their incorporation into the base for employee and employer National Insurance contributions, and this is taken up in Chapter 8.

A form of fringe benefit that the present government has sought to encourage is that of share option schemes and profit-sharing schemes, and this was a major theme of the 1989 Budget. Share option schemes allow employees to buy the company's shares at a stipulated fixed price in the future, amounting to a one-way bet. Under approved share option schemes, there is no tax charge when the option is granted providing that the stipulated price plus any cost of the option is not manifestly less than the current market value, and there is no tax charge when the option is exercised. They are all taxed as capital gains and this only arises when the shares are sold. Under a registered profit-sharing scheme, half of any payment may be made free of tax, up to a limit of £4,000. We do not believe that tax deductibility is necessary to encourage this kind of scheme nor do we consider it defensible on equity grounds. We recommend that these provisions be repealed.

Minimum tax/maximum allowance

A minimum tax has been in effect in the United States since 1969 and it was strengthened as part of the 1986 tax reform, a feature which attracted little attention in Britain. For the personal income tax, it means that taxpayers pay the higher of their regular tax liability or their minimum tax liability. The minimum tax is calculated by taking ordinary taxable income and then adding back allowable deductions (like share options). The minimum tax is then 20 per cent, with exemptions for those with incomes below $150,000. The effect is to stop wealthy taxpayers reducing their liability below 20 per cent and the revenue generated is substantial.

The basic principle of a minimum contribution to the costs of financing the state is one that would command wide acceptance, and as a policy clearly designed to prevent unacceptable levels of avoidance it should attract popular support. In the British context, it is perhaps better cast in terms of a maximum allowance, under which a cash amount per year would set the limit for the total allowances and reliefs that could be claimed by an individual. The advantage of this approach over a minimum tax is that the relationship between the maximum allowance and the personal allowance would be clear.

In our view, the case for a minimum tax or maximum allowance is less strong in Britain than in the United States — providing that tax exemptions are curtailed as we have recommended. But should the base broadening measures turn out to be less effective than hoped, for example due to the operations of the avoidance industry, then we recommend that a maximum allowance or minimum tax be considered to buttress the specific measures.

Conclusions

The income tax base should be broadened, to allow a given revenue to be raised with lower rates, and to treat more fairly different kinds of income. This base broadening would continue the phasing out of mortgage interest relief, as under the Conservatives, would limit all lump sum payments under occupational pensions, would introduce a special tax on the income of pension funds, and would eliminate a whole series of tax exemptions (private medical insurance, Business Expansion Schemes, Personal Equity Plans, share options and profit-sharing schemes). Serious consideration should be given to the introduction of a maximum allowance to limit the total benefit from remaining tax privileges.

Chapter 8

National Insurance contributions

Introduction

This chapter deals first with contributions by the employed and self-employed; employer contributions are taken up towards the end.

Since 1979 the basic rate of income tax has fallen but the rates of National Insurance contribution (NIC) have gone up. The standard rate of Class 1 NIC has risen from 6.5 per cent in 1979 to 9 per cent in 1989. This happened despite the fact that National Insurance benefits have been indexed to prices rather than earnings, which might otherwise have been expected to reduce the contribution burden. One significant reason why there has not been a decline is that the Government has systematically reduced the Treasury Supplement to the National Insurance Fund from the 18 per cent set in the 1975 legislation, and in his 1988 Autumn Statement the Chancellor of the Exchequer announced total abolition of the Supplement. There has been since 1979 a very sizeable switch — nearly £6 billion — in the method of financing. This has helped pay for the cuts in the basic rate of income tax.

Such a transfer in the burden from income tax to NIC might be acceptable if the contributions were a progressive form of taxation. We do indeed see merit in raising revenue in this way, clearly linked to identifiable benefits, and in this chapter we suggest wider use of social security contributions. As it was put in the first Policy Review document *Social Justice and Economic Efficiency*, "paying contributions in return for benefit rights is well understood and receives wide popular acceptance" (page 19). But this is contingent on NIC being converted to a progressive structure. The first section of this chapter shows how the present NIC fails to be progressive and that — despite the 1989 Budget — for many lower paid workers NIC are of the same order of importance as income tax.

It is Labour Party policy, re-affirmed in the Policy Review, to restructure the pattern of NIC on the grounds that:

> *"Despite the changes introduced in the recent budget, National Insurance contributions remain regressive"* (Meet the Challenge, Make the Change, *page 33*).

The second section of this chapter describes how NIC can be restructured. The reform involves contributions only being paid on earnings above the threshold, converting the system into one parallel to the income tax, and the abolition of the upper earnings limit for employees. It also involves the introduction of a social security tax on investment income above a threshold level, and this is described in the third section, together with the proposal to extend the NIC base to include fringe benefits.

The restructuring of NIC raises a number of issues which are considered in the fourth section, together with certain related matters. These are the implications for contribution conditions for benefits, the role of the Treasury Supplement, and whether NIC should be deductible for income tax purposes.

The fifth section of the chapter deals with employer contributions.

Present structure of NIC

The structure of NIC post-October 1989 is such that employees pay Class 1 contributions at the following rates:

- nothing if they earn less than £43 a week;
- £0.86 (2 per cent of £43) plus 9 per cent of their earnings in excess of £43 a week if they earn between £43 and £325;
- £26.24 if they earn more than £325 a week.

These rates apply to employees not contracted out of the state earnings related pension (SERPS). If they are contracted out, being covered by an occupational scheme or by a personal pension, contributions are reduced by 2 per cent of earnings in excess of £43 a week, with a maximum reduction of £5.64 a week. Those who have taken out a personal pension plan, not having been in a contracted-out job for two or more years, benefit from an additional reduction of 2 per cent for 6 years up to 5 April 1993. Finally, certain married women and widows have retained the right to pay reduced rate contributions, currently at the rate of 3.85 per cent.

For the self-employed, there are Class 2 contributions of £4.25 a week (except where earnings are below £2,350 a year) and Class 4 contributions levied at a rate of 6.3 per cent on profits between £5,050 and £16,900 a year. Income tax relief is allowed on 50 per cent of Class 4 contributions. For those with both earned income and self-employment income, there are maxima which limit the total contributions paid.

The need to make the NIC structure progressive has been recognised by the Government. In his 1985 Budget Mr Lawson introduced reduced rate bands, with rates of 5 per cent and 7 per cent at lower earnings levels, and in the 1989 Budget he replaced these by a rate of 2 per cent on earnings below the lower earnings threshold. These measures have meant that the proportion of earnings paid in NIC now rises with earnings — but only up to the upper earnings limit. The continued existence of the upper earnings limit means that NIC fall short of being fully progressive, as is illustrated by the following examples:

- Chief executive earning £200,000 (£3,846 a week)

  pays £26.24 a week (or 0.7%)
- Senior tax manager earning £50,000 (£962 a week)

  pays £26.24 a week (or 2.7%)
- University professor earning £23,380 a year (£450 a week)

  pays £26.24 a week (or 5.8%)
- Supply teacher earning £225 a week

  pays £17.24 a week (or 7.7%)
- Inland Revenue inspector earning £162 a week

  pays £11.57 a week (or 7.1%)
- Coach driver earning £140 a week

  pays £9.59 a week (or 6.9%)
- Production worker earning £100 a week

  pays £5.99 a week (or 6.0%)
- Home help earning £48 a week

  pays £1.31 a week (or 2.8%)
- Cleaner earning £18 a week

  pays nothing (or 0%).

In practice, some of these people (such as the university professor and the Inland Revenue inspector) would be contracted out, being covered by occupational or personal pension schemes; the figures given above are the full not contracted out rates. But the examples are sufficient to show how the proportion paid in NIC declines quite markedly above the upper earnings limit, with the professor paying a smaller percentage than the supply teacher. (The maximum percentage paid is

Chart 8.1: Earnings distribution and employees NIC schedule

Full-time employees on adult rates April 1989

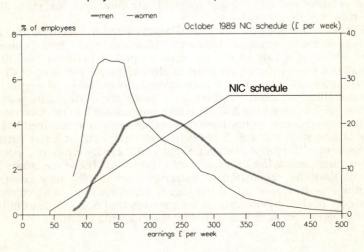

8.1 per cent at the upper earnings limit.)

Whereas the great majority of full-time workers on adult rates are in the range where the standard NIC rate is payable, about 1 in 5 men and 1 in 20 women are above the upper earnings limit of £325 per week — see Chart 8.1. Moreover, the upper earnings limit has risen less rapidly than top earnings: since April 1979 it has increased by about 140 per cent, compared with a rise of some 180 per cent in the top decile of male earnings. This means that more people now fall in the regressive section of the schedule.

Despite the reductions at the bottom of the scale, NIC remains a substantial burden on lower paid workers, as may be seen by comparing NIC with the income tax paid. If the production worker were married to the home help, they would pay (in 1989/90) £3.97 in income tax, but £7.30 in NIC. A married worker pays more NIC than income tax on earnings up to £112.50 a week, and in any case we have argued that the income tax burden on the low paid is too high.

It is also the case that the lower earnings limit generates a "spike" where £1 increase in earnings triggers a disproportionate increase in NIC liability: moving from £42 to £43 costs £0.86. This is less serious than the jump to paying the full 9 per cent on £43 which used to apply, or the sequence of spikes with the reduced rates introduced in 1985, but nonetheless may act as a deterrent to increasing earnings. It is particularly relevant to part-time workers.

The impact of NIC on lower paid workers will be affected by the minimum wage, to which Labour is committed, with an eventual target of ⅔ of median earnings for adult males. This would have major implications, particularly for women workers, and it should be borne in mind that the distribution of earnings may be rather different from that under the Conservatives.

A fully progressive NIC structure

We recommend that the NIC structure be made fully progressive by abolishing the upper earnings limit and by charging a zero rate on earnings below the earnings threshold. The first of these changes would ensure that the proportion paid in contributions would rise steadily with earnings; the second change would reduce the burden proportionately more for the low paid.

The new schedule would be more like that for income tax, but we do not recommend the full integration of NIC with income tax. While it would be possible to hypothecate part of the income tax revenue as a contribution to National Insurance, there are several reasons against this step:

- it would weaken public perception of the insurance basis and reduce the degree of popular acceptance;
- it would appear to raise the basic rate of income tax;
- the base would be reduced by present deductions from taxable income, such as mortgage interest;
- contributions would become payable by pensioners.

The main advantage is that the base would be extended to include investment income, and we consider below the introduction of a social security tax on investment income received by those below retirement age.

The impact of our proposals for employee contributions is to reduce the burden of NIC at lower earnings levels and increase it at higher earnings, the break-even point being above the present upper earnings limit. As may be seen from Chart 8.1, this means that the great majority of those paying more had the fully progressive structure been in force in April 1989 would be men working full-time, paid at adult rates. The reform would redistribute towards generally low paid female workers.

As far as contributions by the self-employed are concerned, the Class 4 contributions are already graduated, in that they are only payable on the excess of profits over the lower threshold. We would make them fully progressive in the same way as Class 1 by abolishing the upper limit (which would also mean that there was no maximum for contributions under Classes 1 and 4 combined). In the case of Class 2 contributions, the fact that they are only payable where earnings reach a specified level leads to a spike at this point. We recommend that they be replaced by a lower starting point for Class 4 contributions, which we would align with that for Class 1, and an increase in the Class 4 rate. This simplification of the schedules would particularly benefit the less well-off self-employed.

Extending the base for social security contributions

NIC are payable on earned incomes rather than income as assessed for income tax. This raises two questions. The first is the definition of earned incomes, which, with the abolition of the upper earnings limit for employees as well as for employers, is likely to become an even more acute issue. A particular cause for concern is the use of fringe benefits to avoid NIC. The second is the extension of the tax base to non-earned incomes.

In the case of fringe benefits, the issue of avoidance is important. As it is put by Tolley's *National Insurance Contributions 1987-88*, there is

> "a point of major departure between the calculation of earnings for income tax and for contribution purposes, for income tax is assessable on perquisites as well as on other income. It follows, therefore, that it will often be of advantage to both employer and employee if the employee is provided with benefits in kind rather than paid actual remuneration"
> (Section 27.10).

There appears to be no reason in principle or on grounds of fairness why the treatment should be different. We therefore recommend that the treatment of benefits in kind for NIC purposes should be identical to that under income taxation. This would mean, for example, that the benefits from company cars, assessed under the Inland Revenue scale charges, would become subject to NIC.

As far as non-earned income is concerned, we did not feel that NIC should be charged on social security benefits or on occupational pensions; nor did we consider that NIC should be paid on other income received by those over the minimum state pension age. We did not however consider it justified that earned incomes should be subject to NIC but investment income bear no corresponding tax. We therefore recommend the introduction of a social security tax, say at the Class 1 National Insurance contribution rate, payable by those aged under pensionable age on investment income in excess of a specified level. The exemption level would ensure that the small saver was not penalised. This would be the counterpart of NIC but would not convey entitlement to further benefits (in which respect it would be similar to contributions paid on earnings above the upper earnings limit). Investment income would be defined for this purpose as under the investment income surcharge in force up to 1983/4.

Other changes in NIC

(1) Contribution conditions

The restructuring of NIC for employees and the self-employed described above means that there have to be consequential changes in the basis for calculating the contribution conditions for benefits. This is not the place to discuss these conditions, which raise significant issues of social policy. For the present we need only note that changes in the contribution schedule may be "decoupled" from the contribution requirements. A separation of the contributions taken into account for the purposes of calculating benefit entitlement for those actually paid has already been made by the Government in the Social Security Act 1985 to accommodate the introduction of the reduced rates of NIC at that time. In the calculation of the earnings factor relevant to the contribution conditions (and which determines the amount of SERPS eligibility), contributions paid at the reduced rates of 5 per cent and 7 per cent were deemed to be equivalent to contributions paid at the full 9 per cent rate.

(2) The Treasury Supplement

The Conservative Government has successively reduced the Treasury Supplement, and has now announced its abolition. The 1975 legislation provided for a Supplement equal to 18 per cent of the contributions to the National Insurance Fund (before allowing for the contracted-out contribution reductions). At the level of contribution income forecast by the Government Actuary for 1988/9 (Cm 257, Appendix 4), this would have amounted to some £5.7 billion.

The reduction in the Treasury Supplement has been criticised by Labour, and with the present structure of NIC such criticism seems well merited. However, with the fully progressive structure proposed here, the position would be different. Indeed, National Insurance contributions have advantages as a source of revenue in that they appear to be less unpopular than other taxation and strengthen the link between taxes and benefits. We do not therefore recommend the re-introduction of the Treasury Supplement.

(3) Tax deductibility of NIC

When the National Insurance scheme was introduced, relief was provided against income tax for contributions. This relief was reduced in 1949 when short-term benefits ceased to be taxable, and abolished in 1965, being replaced by an increase in the personal allowance. Now that short-term benefits are again taxable, it may be argued that tax deductibility should be re-introduced, particularly on the grounds that it would put the state scheme on the same basis as private schemes (the same effect could be achieved by making the contribution into one paid entirely by employers, although this would depend on the consequent adjustments in gross wages).

It has however to be remembered that contributions are now income-related, rather than flat-rate as in 1948, and that the value of tax deductibility would be to reduce the net contribution by more for higher rate taxpayers and by zero for those below the tax threshold. It is not clear that this would be desirable on distributional grounds, and it would be even less so if the income tax structure becomes graduated as we have proposed. We do not therefore recommend that NIC be tax deductible and on the same basis we propose the abolition of the 50 per cent deductibility for Class 4 contributions.

Employer National Insurance contributions

The present (October 1989) structure of National Insurance contributions for employers has retained the reduced rate bands. For workers who are not contracted out, the employer has to pay secondary Class 1 contributions:

- nothing if the worker earns less than £43 a week;
- 5% of earnings if the worker earns between £43 and £74.99 a week;
- 7% of earnings if the worker earns between £75 and £114.99 a week;
- 9% of earnings if the worker earns between £115 and £164.99 a week;
- 10.45% of earnings if the worker earns more than £115 a week.

There is no upper earnings limit for employer contributions. Where the worker is contracted out, contributions are reduced by 3.8 per cent of earnings in excess of £43 a week up to £325 a week.

The contributions by employers have received less attention than those by employees, but they are certainly in need of reform. In particular, the present structure involves "spikes" as the reduced rate bands are crossed. This means that a small increase in pay may trigger a larger increase in National Insurance contributions. Moving from £42 to £43 costs the employer an additional £2.15 since he has to begin paying contributions; moving from £74 to £75 costs an additional £1.55, since the rate of 7 per cent becomes payable on all earnings. There is quite a high penalty to crossing the thresholds. They provide a disincentive for employers to raise earnings above these levels and have been seen as one of the factors leading employers to restrict the hours of employment offered.

In order to avoid this, it is necessary to replace the trigger system by a *slice* system such that the rate is only payable on the slice of earnings above the threshold. We recommend that the contribution schedule be modified to be of the same form as proposed for employees, with a single rate (corresponding to the current rate of 10.45 per cent) levied on all earnings above the lower earnings limit. Moving from £42 to £43 would then mean that no additional contributions were paid and they would become chargeable only on earnings in excess of £43. There would no longer be a strong financial incentive to keep workers below the level at which they can enter the National Insurance system.

In the case of both employee and employer contributions, it is necessary to consider the impact of proposed changes on wage levels and the labour market. Equally, account needs to be taken of the extent to which re-structuring of NIC could facilitate the introduction of the minimum wage. For employees, it is the top end of the scale which is most affected, through the abolition of the upper earnings limit. This may lead to pressure to recoup through wage increases some of the burden of increased contributions, in which case the effect may show up in part in higher prices. On the employer side, the restructuring would provide an incentive for employers to take on lower paid workers. The cost in terms of NIC of employing two workers at £200 a week would (with a threshold of £43 and a rate of 10.45 per cent) be £32.81 compared with £41.80, the cost of employing one worker on £400. This, coupled with the removal of the incentive to "bunch" workers at the NIC thresholds, may well operate in the direction of expanding employment opportunities for the low paid. This is a natural complement of Labour's policy to provide pathways out of poverty.

As with employee contributions, the base should be extended to include fringe benefits. The administration of National Insurance contributions needs also to be considered. The Low Pay Unit has drawn attention to the prevalence of non-payment by employers. This means not only that revenue is not collected but also that the employees concerned are not entitled to benefits. In only a small percentage of cases where NIC irregularities are discovered is the employer subject to prosecution, and the enforcement activities of the Department of Social Security appear to be given lower priority than those dealing with fraudulent claims for benefit. We recommend that enforcement activities on contributions be given the same importance as those on the benefit side.

Conclusions

The restructuring of National Insurance contributions should be taken considerably further than in the 1989 Budget, so that both employee and employer contributions are paid only on earnings above the threshold and that the upper earnings limits for employee and employer contributions are abolished. Fringe benefits should be added to the base for employee and employer contributions. A social security tax on investment income in excess of a threshold should be introduced for those under pension age.

Chapter 9

Capital taxation

In this chapter we consider the taxation of capital gains and of capital. Capital gains (and losses) should, according to the "ideal" definition of income, be included in the base for income taxation, and this — bipartisan — approach is the one we adopt here in the first section. The second section of the chapter deals with the taxation of capital, paying particular attention to the taxation of capital transfers, that is wealth that is passed on at death through bequests or that is given away during a person's lifetime.

Capital gains and losses

Capital gains, or the increases in the value of assets, fall within the comprehensive definition of income. In our view they should be taxed as far as possible in the same way as other income. There is no reason in equity to distinguish between that part of the return to shares which is paid out as a dividend and that part which accrues to the shareholder through a rise in the share price; and the existence of differential tax treatment has had in the past a seriously distorting effect on financial and other decisions. The receipt of income in the form of capital appreciation has been traditionally a major plank in investment advice for the wealthy.

The fact that capital gains should in principle be treated in the same way as other investment income was recognised by Mr Lawson in his 1988 Budget Speech (it is for this reason that we refer to the approach as "bipartisan"):

"*In principle, there is little economic difference between income and capital gains ... And, insofar as there is a difference, it is by no means clear why one should be taxed more heavily than the other*" (Hansard, *15 March 1988*)

He went on in his 1988 Budget to replace the previous flat-rate capital gains tax rate of 30 per cent by the taxpayer's own marginal rate. We recommend that this be retained with the graduated rate structure proposed here. There are however several respects in which capital gains enjoys privileged treatment relative to other investment income, and in our judgement Mr Lawson did not go far enough.

The relative advantages for capital gains include:

● the indexation of capital gains, so that tax is only levied on the real return;

- the exemption of the first £5,000 of chargeable gains;
- retirement relief is given on the sale of certain business assets by persons aged 60 or over;
- the exemption of gains on owner-occupied housing, on most UK corporate bonds and on government securities;
- the postponement of taxation on gains until they are realised through the sale of assets, and roll-over relief for certain assets;
- the exemption of capital gains on death;
- deferment of tax in the case of certain gifts where holdover relief continues to apply.

The first of these (indexation) has already been discussed; the others are taken up in turn below.

In recommending that capital gains be treated, as far as possible, in the same way as other investment income, we are not proposing that the two tax bases be combined, with tax being applied to the sum of all investment income plus capital gains. If that were done, then capital losses could be set against interest and dividend income (or indeed against earned income). If we continue to apply a realisation basis, rather than an accrual basis, as proposed below, then it would be possible for the investor to realise losses artificially in order to reduce the tax due on interest and dividends. In order to prevent this, we would allow losses only to be set against capital gains, as at present. (In the US Tax Reform Act of 1986 which integrated income and capital gains taxation, a limit of $3,000 was placed on net capital losses which could be set against other income.) In the same way, our proposal in Chapter 8 for a social security tax on investment income envisages that this additional rate would also apply to chargeable capital gains, but again losses may be set only against capital gains (not other investment income).

The exemption of the first £5,000 of gains (after the tax changes for husband and wife in 1990 it will apply to each of them) has no apparent justification in equity, and in principle we would like to see all gains taxed in the same way as other income. We accept however that for administrative reasons it is necessary to have a *de minimis* exemption; we recommend that this be set at a substantially lower level than at present — for example, a fifth of the present level — although we realise that the precise level must take account of the balance between extra revenue and administrative cost. This will take further the process set in train by Mr Lawson when he reduced the annual exemption from £6,600 to £5,000 in 1988. Furthermore, it should be noted that the level at which it was set in 1965, of £50 per year, would be less than £400 in current prices.

Associated with the annual exemption is the retirement relief. This exempts gains on the disposal of a business or of shares in a family company for persons aged 60 or over and for those retiring on grounds of ill-health, with the first £125,000 of gains being completely exempt and half of gains between £125,000 and £500,000. One of the justifications for this relief is that the owner of a unincorporated business may not be able to take advantage of the annual exemption, in that the disposal has to take place in a single transaction at retirement. By the same token, the reduction in the annual exemption means that the retirement relief need be nothing like as generous. Other justifications include that of providing an incentive for disposal on retirement, so that businessmen do not hold on to the ownership after retirement so as to postpone capital gains tax liability. This may be significant at present with the exemption of gains at death, but we propose below making gains chargeable on death. Moreover, the retirement relief provides a *dis*-incentive to businessmen planning to sell *before* retirement.

After considering these, and other incentive arguments, the IFS Capital Taxes Group concluded that "in our view retirement relief should now be substantially reduced or abolished altogether" (*Death: The Unfinished Business*, 1988, page 33). Bearing in mind that the introduction of the graduated rate structure will impose a penalty on the realisation of gains in a block, rather than spread over time, we do not recommend complete abolition. Instead we recommend that the relief be reduced by the same proportion as the annual exemption.

One very important class of assets which is exempt from capital gains tax is principal private residences. The Inland Revenue estimate that the tax collected in 1987/8 would have been £6 billion if no roll-over relief were permitted (*Inland Revenue Statistics 1988*, Table 1.6). Of course, they recognise that this is an over-estimate in that the introduction of a capital gains tax charge would undoubtedly lead to a fall in house prices, eliminating part of the capital gain. It is difficult to estimate the magnitude of this effect. Moreover, any proposal to abolish the exemption of owner-occupied houses would probably include provisions for roll-over relief, exempting proceeds re-invested in a principal private residence within a specified period. This would mean that the liability would in most cases be postponed until the person moved to a smaller house or until death. As a result, the revenue collected would only be some small fraction of the £6 billion figure.

The IFS Capital Taxes Group recommend that capital gains tax be extended to gains on principal private residences, which they say "are widely perceived as an unmerited accretion of wealth which could be fairly taxed" (1988, page 2). Their proposal involves roll-over relief and a separate, higher threshold for these assets. While we understand the logic of their argument, we believe that it would be politically impossible for the Labour Party to advocate the removal of capital gains tax exemption for owner-occupiers in general and we do not recommend that this step be taken. Although the tax liability would in fact in most cases be postponed until death, or at least old age, it would be perceived as a threat to younger home-owners and, to the extent that it was capitalised in lower house prices, it would have an immediate impact on their net worth. In our view the better route to follow is more effective taxation of capital transfers, and this is discussed below. At the same time, there may be cases where the exemption is being abused by people who are effectively trading through moving house frequently in order to make speculative gains, and this may need further consideration.

In Chapter 4 we described the difference between taxing capital gains as they accrue, which is the basis indicated by the "ideal" definition of income, and the actual taxation on realisation, which means that tax is postponed and the investor in effect receives an interest-free loan from the Revenue until realisation. Not only does this reduce the effective tax paid on capital gains relative to other kinds of investment income, but also it has a "lock-in" effect. An investor may be deterred from selling an asset to buy another on account of the fact that this sale would bring forward the capital gains tax liability: he is locked in to his portfolio. This may adversely affect the working of the capital market. In the case of business assets, the problem is met by the roll-over relief which allows postponement where the proceeds are re-invested in a business asset within a specified period.

The advantage from postponement could be offset if the tax rate levied were increased according to the length of the holding period. The Meade Committee suggested a formula such that the tax charged on realisation approximated that due on an accrual basis. There are clearly considerable administrative costs in such a scheme and we do not consider it a high priority. Moreover, the introduction of the graduated rate structure will provide some incentive for the smoothing of capital gains realisation over time. We therefore accept that the present realisation basis for capital gains will continue.

We do not however accept that gains should be exempt from capital gains tax on death. At present there is no liability to capital gains tax on the assets which form part of a person's estate and those who acquire the assets are deemed to have acquired them at their market value at the date of death. The tax is therefore foregone, not merely postponed. We can see no justification for this exemption and recommend that capital gains tax be charged at death on the basis that the assets were realised at that date. This would return to the position when the tax was introduced by the Labour Government in 1965. This would not apply to assets transferred to a surviving spouse, when holdover relief would apply. According to the Inland Revenue estimate, the revenue lost through the exemption was £175 million in 1987/8, although allowance has to be made for the interaction with inheritance taxation, since the estate would be reduced by the amount of the capital gains tax liability.

We believe that the deferment of capital gains tax in the case of gifts should be limited, except in the case of gifts to a spouse where it should continue. In the case of business assets we suggest that consideration be given to the beneficiary having a range of options, including immediate payment, phased payments, or the issue of shares to an appropriate publicly nominated body. The aim of these arrangements would be to allow the business to continue while preventing a situation where the payment of taxation was deferred without limit. The relief for political parties should be abolished.

Capital gains tax: conclusions

Like Mr Lawson, we believe that capital gains should be taxed at the rate applicable to other income, but we propose that the annual exemption, and retirement relief, should be reduced very substantially and that capital gains tax should be charged at death.

Capital taxation

The Committee considered the general question of a new tax on capital against the background of the fact that the decline in the concentration of wealth in Britain which characterised earlier decades has come to a virtual stop in the 1980s. The official estimates of the distribution of marketable wealth show that the bottom 50 per cent of the adult population in 1986 owned a mere 7 per cent of individual net wealth (*Inland Revenue Statistics 1988*, Table 10.5). Measures to achieve a more equitable distribution of wealth in Britain are very necessary.

The form which such measures should take is however more debatable. The Committee recognised that there is a case for the introduction of an explicit annual wealth tax, but at the same time saw that there are difficulties in determining the base for such a tax and the level of wealth at which it would become payable. The introduction of a wealth tax would absorb considerable legislative and administrative resources and the Committee did not feel that it should be given priority over other reforms advocated here, particularly those designed to make the taxation of investment income more effective. The Committee is also of the view that the most pressing area for reform in the field of capital taxation is that concerning inherited wealth, which remains a very considerable cause of inequality.

The Committee therefore decided to concentrate in this Report on the reform of existing taxes on capital transfers.

Capital transfer taxation

In 1974 the Labour Government introduced *capital transfer tax* with the aim of taxing the total wealth transferred by a person over his or her lifetime in the form of gifts or bequests. It replaced the old estate duty which was limited to gifts made within 7 years of death, and in principle it should have provided the basis for effective taxation of wealth transfers. But the principle was eroded by amendments during Labour's period of office and since 1979 its teeth have largely been drawn by the Conservatives. There is no bipartisan approach to capital transfer taxation. The 1981 Budget ended lifetime cumulation, replacing it by a 10 year period, and reduced the top rate on lifetime transfers from 75 per cent to 50 per cent. In 1986 the tax on lifetime gifts was abolished, the tax reverting to one on estates plus gifts made within seven years of death. This reversion to estate duty was marked by the rechristening of the tax as *inheritance tax*. The rate band in 1986 had seven steps from 30 per cent to 60 per cent; this was reduced to four bands in 1987; and further reduced to the single rate of 40 per cent in 1988.

The degree of erosion of capital transfer taxes may be seen from the statistics for revenue. In 1974/5 estate duty — then widely described as a "voluntary tax" — was raising 1.1 per cent of tax revenues; in 1988/9 inheritance tax is forecast to yield 0.7 per cent. Revenue from capital transfer taxation has declined relative to other receipts. The benefit from this has accrued particularly to the very wealthy. A person leaving £1 million in 1978 would have paid, assuming that the full rates were due, CTT of £583,250, which means that the net amount received by the heir was £416,750. A person leaving £3 million in 1989 (this is broadly the same multiple of average earnings) would pay inheritance tax of £1,152,800, leaving £1,847,200. The average tax rate has fallen from 58.3 per cent to 38.5 per cent. If the assets yield 10 per cent, then this is equivalent to an increase in income of over £1,000 a week. Moreover, this calculation assumes that the duty is paid in full and no advantage is taken of the routes for avoidance. As it was put by the IFS Capital Taxes Group:

> "By the use of trusts and by lifetime giving, the very wealthy and well-advised can (if they choose) escape paying much [inheritance tax] at all, and can effectively pass on substantial chunks of wealth tax-free" (Death: The Unfinished Business, 1988, page 23).

On top of the devices mentioned, there are such concessions as the relief of up to 50 per cent for agricultural and business assets, which again reduce the effective tax paid. It is not surprising that inheritance continues to be a major force leading to inequality in the distribution of wealth. To quote again from the IFS Capital Taxes Group, "the sharp reduction in inheritance tax rates directly contributes to sustaining concentrations of wealth in the hands of those whose forebears owned it" (1988, page 25).

The taxation of wealth transfers is not however solely a matter of the very rich. The post-war growth in owner-occupation, and the sale of council houses, together with the large rise in house prices, mean that the inheritance of property is becoming much more common. It is estimated that the inheritance of housing is now worth around £7 billion a year, and that this is likely to increase steadily in real terms. The accumulation of capital in this form enjoys fiscal privileges in excess of those for many other forms of saving, including the exemption from capital gains tax. As we have argued, it would not be easy for Labour to abolish the capital gains tax exemption; for this reason we see the introduction of more effective taxation of capital transfers as an essential counter-weight.

Return to capital transfer tax

There are three main reform possibilities. The first is to return to the capital transfer tax (CTT). This would mean a *donor-based* tax in which the tax is levied on the total transferred by a person in lifetime gifts plus the estate at death. It would be progressive with respect to this total. Suppose that a man gives £25,000 to each of his two children at age 60, and then when he dies at the age of 80 he leaves his house worth £80,000 to his daughter and £35,000 in shares to his son. He would under CTT be taxed on the £50,000 transferred at age 60 and then tax would be due on his estate at the rate applicable to the next £115,000.

We would envisage that under a revised CTT the starting point would be relatively high, as with the current inheritance tax, but the rate schedule would be graduated. Rather than the present single 40 per cent rate, there would be rates rising from, say, 10 per cent to 60 per cent steps. (The CTT schedule introduced by Denis Healey went from 10 per cent to 75 per cent, reaching the top rate on transfers of £2 million or more.) One consequence of this reform is that less would be paid by estates which are currently not far above the present threshold of £118,000. The loss of revenue on such amounts of wealth, which may simply be the value of an owner-occupied house being left to the children, will be offset by the increased amounts paid on estates valued in millions and on those lifetime transfers which currently escape.

The base for the new CTT would need to be considered, particularly in the light of the erosion of the base which accompanied the earlier attempt to introduce effective transfer taxation. The view of the Committee is that there should be no special exemptions for business or farming assets, although there should be arrangements for payment which ensure the stability of small businesses and farms. These arrangements would for example allow the payment of CTT in instalments. There would continue to be exemption of transfers to charities.

A lifetime capital receipts tax

An alternative to returning to CTT is to introduce a new *donee-based* tax. This would be levied on the total of wealth transfers *received* over a specified period, which could be the lifetime of the individual. This would mean, in our example, that the daughter would be taxed on the receipt of £105,000 in total and the son on £60,000. We refer to this kind of tax as a *lifetime capital receipts tax*.

One of the major advantages claimed for the lifetime capital receipts tax (LCRT) is that it would provide an incentive for donors to leave their wealth to people who have received little in the way of transfers. The man in our hypothetical example may have left more to his daughter because his son had already received money from his father-in-law. With a donor-based system, like CTT, no account would be taken of wealth inherited from other sources; with the LCRT the tax rate paid by the son would have been higher. (It is of course possible that the donor would have been sufficiently long-sighted to recognise that under the CTT his son would pay more duty when he in turn came to pass on the wealth, but it seems unlikely that this would weigh as heavily.) Moreover, if our concern is with large inheritances, then it appears natural to tax directly the object of concern.

The design of a new LCRT raises several issues. First, the *unit* of assessment should clearly be the individual, but the Committee felt that inter-spousal transfers should be exempt on the basis that transfers should be taxed only once a generation. Secondly, there would have to be an annual exemption for receipts on a *de minimis* basis. Thirdly, the switch from a donor to a recipient basis would multiply the number of individuals with whom the Revenue would have to deal, although the information about donees would be available, in the case of transfers at death, from the probate records. In order to ease the collection problems, it is proposed that a *withholding tax* be levied on estates in excess of a specified amount. The tax withheld would then be credited against the LCRT due to be paid by recipients and would be refunded where no tax was due. The base for the LCRT would be defined in a similar way to that for CTT. Transfers to charities would continue to be tax-free. Finally, there is the question of transfers to those not domiciled in the UK. The withholding rate would be charged in these cases.

Taxing transfers as income

The principle underlying the *lifetime capital receipts tax* regards wealth transfers as equivalent to other additions to purchasing power. We could indeed treat gifts or bequests received as adding to a person's stock of resources in the same way as earnings, and a third direction for reform would be to tax capital transfers received as income. This is proposed by the IFS Capital Taxes Group, who recommend that the amount of capital received in transfers each year be added to a person's total income and taxed according to the income tax schedule. They would allow an annual exemption, as for capital gains, so that, whatever their level of income, people could receive a certain amount of gifts and or bequests before they became chargeable. It should be noted that their recommendation is based on the assumption of the present income tax structure; it is not clear that they would maintain the recommendation if the rate structure became graduated as we have proposed. It should however be noted that the tax rate proposed here of 50 per cent is only 10 per cent higher than the current inheritance tax rate. (We do not envisage that capital transfers would be subject to the additional social security tax.) In practical terms, we might want to allow averaging. The administrative difficulties mean however that this is not done on any extensive scale for the income tax (one exception being the Schedule D assessment of farms and market gardens); and we feel that these may also be decisive for capital receipts, particularly given the very natural concern that people have about the accumulation of information by central government.

Conclusions

The Committee recommends strongly that reform of capital transfer taxation should be carried out by the next Labour Government. It has a preference for a recipient-based tax, either the *lifetime capital receipts tax* or that gifts and bequests should be charged to income tax. It would however also regard a return to an effective capital transfer tax as a realistic option.

Chapter 10

Business and corporate taxes

We have been concentrating so far on the taxing of individuals; we turn now to the taxation of business. Businesses can be subject to income tax if conducted by individuals, or to corporation tax if conducted by companies. In this chapter we consider first the income tax treatment of business income, and then go on to examine the corporation tax regime for companies. The latter is of particular importance. Despite the growth in the numbers engaged in self-employment — an extra 1 million since 1981 — the bulk of business activity is conducted by companies. Moreover, we have to bear in mind that many present-day companies form part of a group operating in a range of territories and encountering many different tax regimes. The international aspects, and steps towards European harmonisation, will therefore play a significant role in our discussion. It should also be noted that we are primarily concerned with the taxation of companies in general, and we do not go into the particular issues which arise in specific sectors, such as banking and financial services, or oil production. Neither do we develop our thoughts on some of the detailed provisions on such matters as, for example, group treatment or debt/equity arrangements where we consider a tightening of the rules to be appropriate.

Sole traders and partnerships

Following our earlier discussion of the income tax base, we find it entirely appropriate that individuals to whom income accrues directly from the operation of a business should be subject to income tax on that income. Income from business sources should be taxed on the same basis as other income. In particular, the self-employed should not obtain any tax advantages when compared with those who are employed.

Under existing legislation, there are two respects in which the self-employed have the benefit of a generally more liberal regime:
(a) there are different rules for the assessment and payment of tax;
(b) the different provisions for the deductibility of expenses.

The basis of assessment differs in that business profits are assessed on a *preceding years basis*. Apart from the early and closing years of a business, the profit assessed is that arising in the accounting year ending in the preceding tax year. If for example a business makes up its accounts to 31 December in any year, then the tax assessable in the tax year 1989/90 would be based on the profits of the business in the year ending 31 December 1988. The tax payable for 1989/90 is due as one half on 1st January 1990 and one half on 1st July 1990. This means that the income used as a basis for assessing tax will have been earned — with a 31 December year end — between 1.5 and 2.5 years before the date at which the final instalment of tax is actually paid.

This procedure is far removed from the PAYE system applied to employees and in general works to the advantage of the self-employed. There is the benefit from having personal allowances and a rate structure which are typically geared to current earnings being applied to unindexed profits. There is the benefit from postponing the tax payment. Moreover, where a business is seasonal, choosing the most appropriate accounting year can defer for as long as possible the tax charge.

The preceding year basis cannot operate for the early years of a business and special rules are adopted which mean that the initial profits can feature in 3 years of assessment. As it is often the case that profits are at their lowest when a business is getting started, this basis can be a considerable tax benefit. Even if it is not, the taxpayer has the right to revert to an actual basis. At the close of business, the Revenue have the right to revise the assessments so that the final 3 years are based on the actual profits earned in those years. However, by careful planning of the date of cessation of a business, the taxpayer can cause a high year of profit to drop out of the tax net.

We recommend that the basis of assessment for business income become a current year basis and that tax be payable on account during the tax year in which the income arises. The practical problem that the final profit figure is not determined until the accounts are finalised does not prevent an initial assessment being made of the profits arising in any tax year with a subsequent adjustment to reflect actual profits. The progress which is being made in the computerisation of assessments should allow this to be done. There will of course have to be transitional provisions for existing businesses. Similarly, on the matter of tax payments, we would wish to see tax being paid on account, with interest being paid where the payment is excessive and charged where additional tax proves to be due.

It should be emphasised that this change is recommended on the grounds that self-employment income should be treated in the same way as other income. As far as the current year basis is concerned, a similar change was made in the case of bank interest income in 1985. We do not wish to discourage self-employment, and we believe that the self-employed may welcome the greater certainty and clarity of tax liability which the proposed system would make possible.

The basis under which expenses can be deducted from employment income has been discussed in Chapter 7. For employees, the narrow rule is, as we noted in Chapter 7, that relief for expenditure is given "if the holder of .... employment is *necessarily* obliged to incur ... the expenses of travelling in the performance of the duties of the ... employment, or of keeping and maintaining a horse to enable him to perform those duties, or otherwise to expend money *wholly, exclusively and necessarily* in the performance of those duties..." (*Income and Corporation Taxes Act 1988*, 198(1), our italics). Although at the margins this fairly rigorous rule has been sensibly interpreted through "extra statutory concessions", it has served to limit strictly the expenses which may be deducted from emoluments in calculating the amount assessable to tax. In Chapter 7 we concluded that this rigorous rule should be retained.

Self-employed people, on the other hand, face the test that expenditure must only be *wholly and exclusively* expended for the purpose of the business. There is no requirement that it must be *necessarily* incurred. Moreover, the *wholly* is generally interpreted as determining "how much" and as not denying relief where only part relates to a business. The *exclusively* requirement often does not in practice deny relief where there is duality of purpose for expenditure but an accurate apportionment of a business element can be made.

It may reasonably be argued that to align the rules for business deductions with those applying for employments, and to introduce the *necessarily incurred* test, would be impracticable. Even for small businesses the ability to incur expenditure may not be vested solely in the proprietor, and the process of making judgments in a whole range of situations as to whether any expenditure was necessary would be administratively difficult. Nonetheless, we believe that the position should be the subject of a review by the Inland Revenue, with a view to a more equitable treatment of expenses deducted by the self-employed, particularly in areas where the expenditure is also of personal benefit to the proprietor or his or her family.

One major area of potential unfairness which should be considered by this review is that which arises at present with those who are treated as self-employed but whose circumstances so far as place of work, nature of duties, degree of responsibility may differ little from those who are employed. A chartered accountant employed at a professional office in the City would get no relief for the costs of fares to and from work. Her counterpart, self-employed and nominally based at home, making a similar regular journey to two or three accounting firm clients where sub-contract work was undertaken, would get travel costs allowed. At the margins, the unfairness is clearly visible. The recent article in the *Employment Gazette* showed that of some 3 million self-employed members of the labour force, about two-thirds employ nobody else directly (see Curran and Burrows (1989)). General Household Survey data suggest that a third of men in this category operated in construction whereas for women the "other services" classification was the main area of self-employment. We believe that there is scope for a more restrictive definition of expenses which may be deductible in some of these situations. Travel costs, home expenses and clothing allowances are items which require particular attention.

In part, this review may be necessary for other reasons. As technology develops, the opportunity for people to work from their home increases and, just as proposals are being developed to achieve a more comprehensive structure for employment rights and protection in these changing circumstances, so will an overhaul be necessary of the distinctions between those who are treated as employed and as self-employed.

In the interim, proposals of the Labour Party on such issues as low pay, employment rights and training opportunities will, if enacted, of themselves encourage more people to embrace an employment contract rather than the existing tax benefits of self-employment.

Incorporation

The potential tax advantages of individuals seeking to incorporate their business is a complex matter involving a weighing of benefits and costs. Incorporation, for example, brings the second tier of taxing capital gains as well as the inability to offset losses against other income. The benefits of being able to shelter from high personal tax rates by accumulating profits within a company and realising them as capital gains has diminished as tax rates have declined and some alignment of income tax rates with those for capital gains has taken place. We also recognise that incorporation is not only undertaken for tax planning purposes, and that indeed these may play no role. Limited liability can still be an important commercial benefit, although it is accompanied by obligations on financial reporting, and may in the future carry more onerous obligations if the thrust of company law enlarges the responsibility of directors.

At the same time, we must take account of the fact that the proposals outlined in earlier chapters may lead to tax planning via incorporation. An important safeguard will, in our view, be a revamped close company regime. (The previous provisions were largely dismantled in the 1989 Finance Act.) This should have the triple objective of:

(i) not allowing expenses to be deducted for a company which would not have been allowed for the individual;

(ii) not allowing benefits to be obtained from the company in a non-taxable form;

(iii) not allowing resources to be sheltered or deferred from higher personal income tax and national insurance rates.

The third point is the most difficult area in the case of trading companies where there may be perfectly genuine reasons for retaining funds for reinvestment. We would favour a regime which was not unduly restrictive in discouraging reinvestment but not so general as to enable the most facile arguments for retentions to succeed.

Corporate sector

The purpose of the remaining part of this chapter is to examine what, if any, type of system we should have for taxing companies. We begin by describing briefly the present provisions. We go on to review the arguments for a separate company tax and the form which it should take. We then consider some of the key policy issues raised by the current structure.

Since 1965, companies have been subject to corporation tax rather than income tax, and since 1973 have been subject to the *imputation system*. A company for this purpose includes an unincorporated association but excludes partnerships. Broad features of the system include:

(a) Corporation tax is effectively a flat rate tax on company profits, with a lower rate for "small companies". Small companies for this purpose are those with profits of £150,000 or less but with marginal relief for profits up to £750,000.

(b) Part of the company tax liability is imputed to shareholders when dividends are paid so, for example, an individual taxpayer receiving a dividend of £75 gets a *tax credit* of £25 which covers the basic rate liability on the income of £100 (cash dividend plus tax credit). It is referred to as *Advance Corporation Tax* (ACT), although Advance *Income* Tax would be a more accurate description. This system was designed to operate so as to encourage the distribution of profits, although for a period when little corporation tax was paid because of stock relief and capital allowances the ACT paid by many companies became an actual cost rather than an offset at company level.

(c) The exempting from tax of dividends coming from other UK resident companies.

(d) *Grouping* provisions whereby various group companies are allowed to pass losses to each other and generally to distribute profits between themselves free of ACT and to transfer assets free of tax on capital gains.

(e) The retention of the schedular system of income and gains whereby profits are computed separately for trades, income from land, interest income, capital gains, foreign income and miscellaneous income. There is no general co-mingling of such sources although there are defined rules for use of losses.

(f) Profits as defined for tax purposes are derived from the accounting profits shown by company accounts. These accounts are based on historic costs and are not adjusted for inflation.

(g) Although also applicable to income tax, the structure of the tax and case law inherently distinguishes between *capital* and *revenue items*. The latter (eg wages) are generally deductible from taxable profits whereas capital expenditure is sometimes deductible over a period against income, (eg plant and machinery, industrial buildings) and sometimes not deductible in computing income at all (eg. office buildings or goodwill). (However, the costs of these latter items would feature in a capital gains computation on a disposal of such assets.) Where capital assets are depreciable for tax purposes, these allowances are given as *capital allowances* covering machinery and plant, industrial buildings, agricultural buildings, scientific research, mines and oil wells and any accounting depreciation charged in the accounts of the company is displaced by these allowances in the tax computation.

(h) Interest costs are generally deductible in computing profits either as a routine trading item or under special rules against the totality of a company's or group's profit. This, for example, allows interest costs incurred on borrowings to acquire a new group company to be set against the profits of that company.

(i) The period of assessment is an *accounting period* which cannot exceed 12 months. This period is whatever 12 month period a company chooses. Tax, except to the extent generated by ACT, is not payable until at least 9 months after the end of the accounting period.

(j) Corporation tax applies to the worldwide profits of a company which is resident in the UK (subject to giving credit for foreign tax paid to other jurisdictions) and to the branch trading profits of a company operating in, but not resident in, the UK.

Principles of company taxation

The company may be viewed in different ways when considering the underlying principles of taxation. In one view it may be argued that the company is simply a "veil" and that our concern should be with ultimate beneficiaries: ie the shareholders. On this basis, corporate taxation is simply a convenient way of collecting personal income tax which should be due from the shareholders. This argument provides a clear justification for imputation, corporation tax simply being an advance income tax payment. It may also be recognised than income accrues to shareholders in part in the form of capital gains. These enjoy a relatively favoured tax treatment — even if taxed at income tax rates — in view of the annual exemption, the indexation provisions, and the deferral of tax liability until the gains are realised. The imposition of the corporation tax, and the limitation of imputation to a single rate, may then be seen as an approximate offset for the advantages still enjoyed by capital gains.

A second view of the company is that we look at it as a form of collective which has an identity and a succession which is independent of its members, employers and consumers at any one point in time. The company is a person in law and to the extent to which it generates profits it should be required to contribute to government revenues. On this basis, a separate corporate tax is justified and no particular case can be made for imputation. It is not our aim here to decide between these — and other — views of the company. In practice, both appear to have influenced the present corporate tax structure and it now represents some degree of compromise. We do not believe that it would be desirable to depart in any major way from this compromise. To abolish the corporation tax would involve a substantial loss of revenue, even allowing for the retention of ACT. The existence of the tax has already been capitalised in asset values, and its abolition would give rise to windfall gains in a pattern that has no evident distributional merit. Moreover, the international aspects are important. The corporation is the most common trading vehicle around the world and all major trading countries have a regime for taxing corporations on some basis or another. If the UK were to abolish its corporation tax the tax paid by international companies would not inevitably be reduced; the tax may simply accrue to another government.

Base for corporation tax and rate of imputation

It has been argued that the base for the corporation tax should be converted to an expenditure tax, or *flow of funds* basis. This would, for example, base the tax system for companies on charging to tax the total receipts from the sale of goods and services and the sale of capital assets *less* the total purchase of goods and services and of capital assets. (Financial transactions would be excluded in both cases.) In effect, this would abolish interest deductibility and extend 100 per cent allowances to all capital purchases.

We have earlier argued against the adoption of an expenditure tax basis for personal taxation, and for similar reasons we do not favour its adoption for company taxation. Two major considerations are that it would increase the possibilities for *tax planning* and that it would fit uneasily internationally. The scope for manipulation in the light of expected future changes in tax rates has been emphasised in Chapter 4, and we do not regard it as desirable that companies would be able to speculate, on a greater scale than at present, on a change in government. (A Labour Chancellor may, for instance, find that revenue sources dry up on this account.) The international dimension, in a world where most countries retained the present tax base, would raise major issues as to how double taxation treaties would operate and how credit for overseas tax would be obtained for UK companies operating overseas.

Even those convinced of the merits of a cash-flow corporation tax would, we feel, agree that its introduction would represent a major investment of parliamentary and administrative time. We are not of the view that this would be justified. As far as companies themselves are concerned, we believe that they would welcome stability in corporate tax arrangements rather than a radical change which would move the UK out of line with other European countries. The clear, if unremarkable, conclusion from this is that we should stay with a corporation tax system based upon income/profits, computed according to present principles.

If the tax base remains as at present, there is the question of the rate of imputation. As already noted, this depends on the view taken of the appropriate role of company taxation. It also depends on the changes in personal taxation. With the graduated rate structure recommended in Chapter 5, there will not necessarily be an obvious single tax rate to be applied. (The basic rate would be abolished.) In our judgement, there should continue to be imputation at a uniform rate, but that the rate should be set by the Chancellor of the day, bearing in mind the following considerations : (a) the structure of personal tax rates, (b) the extent to which the imputation system involves a transfer to tax-exempt institutions, and (c) the refunds to overseas investors under tax treaties. We would expect the rate of imputation to be rather lower than at present. This would reflect the fact that the changes to the tax treatment of capital gains proposed in Chapter 9 would move the balance against retentions and hence a reduction in the rate of imputation would have an offsetting effect. It would also mean that companies with unrelieved ACT, such as those with large overseas tax liabilities, would be treated more nearly on the same basis as other companies.

International aspects

We cannot look at our tax system in isolation. It interrelates with other tax systems in a number of ways:

(a) It will eventually be affected by EC harmonisation proposals, although the process of harmonisation will be a slow one;

(b) UK controlled companies operate overseas, either through branches or other companies, and the tax charge which they face overseas and on repatriation to the UK will have implications for investment decisions (the rules governing the credit given to UK companies in respect of overseas profits are governed by unilateral provisions as well as by provisions of bi-lateral treaties);

(c) Non-UK controlled companies will operate in the UK either through branches or through subsidiaries and the tax charge they face here, either directly or via repatriation, coupled with the rules in the territory of origin allowing a credit or deduction for UK taxation, will be a major issue in determining their investment into the UK.

In earlier chapters we have touched on international aspects, but these are especially important for companies, which are inherently more mobile than individuals and for whom tax planning may be more easily conducted.

We have earlier emphasised the need to design UK policy with a view to possible developments in this field. We have for example taken this into account in discussing the choice of tax base. At the same time, we are impressed by the dangers of individual countries forming independent fiscal policies and of a downward spiral of tax rates as territories bid against each other to attract corporate investment. Therefore a positive approach to corporate tax harmonisation — covering not just rates but also key features such as the tax base — should be high on the agenda for a Labour Chancellor.

Conclusions

The Committee believes that the argument for stability in corporate tax arrangements outweighs any possible advantages of changes in structure. It recommends that consideration should be given to the rate of imputation and to Britain's role in securing European harmonisation of corporate taxation. To secure equity between the self-employed and employed and greater clarity in tax arrangements, the Committee recommends that the basis of assessment for business income should be the current year, with tax payable on account during the year in which it arises. In addition, there should be a review by the Inland Revenue of the provisions for deductions of business expenses.

Chapter 11

Local taxation and the replacement of the poll tax

One of the key issues facing an incoming Labour government will be to find a way of financing local government to replace the poll tax (Community Charge), a tax which in its unfairness epitomises much of the development of tax policy in the last ten years. Action will be needed immediately to remove some of its very worst features, but it will take some time — possibly the life of a parliament — to establish a long term replacement.

The choice of local taxation system and its effects depend, of course, on the structure of local government — including the relationship between district and county councils and possibilities for regional government or territorial devolution — as well as the overall system of grants from central to local government. It is beyond the scope of this Report to examine these two major topics in detail. Rather, our aim here is to discuss the different options for local taxation and the way in which they would relate to the national tax system, taking account of the kinds of reforms we discuss in other chapters.

We describe a range of options for reform, focussing on the two which have been most discussed — a local income tax and capital value rates. The latter would return to a rating system, but with valuation related to the capital value of housing, this being the only realistic way in which rates could be re-introduced. A return to rental values would involve entirely arbitrary valuations given that — in the absence of a functioning market for rental housing — there is no longer any sensible way of assessing rental values for residential property. By contrast, there is very good information on capital values through the market for owner-occupied housing. Other possibilities which have been canvassed at one time or another, but which we do not pursue any further because they fail to meet the basic criteria for acceptability include the following:

(a) A banded poll tax with different payments by those liable to each national income tax band (as this would create jumps in liability at the start of each tax band and would achieve much less satisfactory results than a local income tax while requiring much of the same administration);

(b) Local sales taxes (because of the problem of "cross border shopping" which would be intense if tax rates varied between local authority areas).

Local government income and expenditure

Until now local government has been financed from three sources: grants from central government, non-domestic rates (on commercial and industrial property) and domestic rates. In addition it makes charges for some of the services it provides and collects rents from its own housing.

Table 11.1 shows the change which has occurred in the last ten years in the relative balance between these sources. Between 1979/80 and 1989/90, local government spending in England and Wales (net of charges and based on budgets) rose by 15 per cent in real terms, distinctly less than the growth in real national income. However, central government grants fell in real terms by 18 per cent. As a result, rates had to rise to make up the gap — non-domestic rates by 59 per cent and domestic rates by 83 per cent (a faster increase because of the decline in value of the grant for *domestic rate relief*). Part of the build-up to the poll tax has therefore been the deliberate shift of the tax burden towards the rates — giving an entirely false impression of the growth of local spending over the decade. As a corollary of this, a key issue for an incoming government will be the extent to which this process should be reversed: central government spending is now £6 billion lower (equivalent to 3.5p off the basic rate of income tax) than it would have been if central grants covered the same proportion of local spending as they did in 1979/80. Put another way, families have lost on rates a lot of what they have gained from the income tax cuts of recent years.

Table 11.1 Local authority income and expenditure 1979-80 and 1989-90 England and Wales (£ billion)

	1979-80 (current prices)	1979-80 (at 1989-90 prices) (a)	1989-90	Percentage change
Total rate and grant borne expenditure	16.0	31.4	36.0	+15
Financed by :				
Change in balances	0.5	1.0	0.6	-36
Central grants (b)	9.5	18.5	15.2	-18
Domestic rates (c)	2.6	5.2	9.5	+83
Non-domestic rates	3.4	6.7	10.7	+59

(a) Adjusted by GDP deflator
(b) Block grant plus specific grants plus domestic rate relief
(c) Apportioned by aggregate rateable values (after allowing for domestic rate relief)

Chart 11.1 shows how the revenue raised from this process was spent, giving the breakdown of projected current local authority spending in 1989/90. It is immediately apparent that education makes up nearly

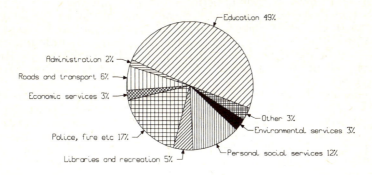

Chart 11.1: Local authority current expenditure by service 1989/90 (England and Wales)

Education 49%

Administration 2%
Roads and transport 6%
Economic services 3%

Other 3%
Environmental services 3%

Police, fire etc 17%

Personal social services 12%

Libraries and recreation 5%

half of the total, and that two thirds is accounted for by education with police, fire, court and probation services. A further key issue discussed below is whether it is appropriate for all this spending to remain the responsibility of local government.

Factors in choosing a local tax

In considering the merits of different kinds of local tax the issues to be considered include:
● ability to pay;
● relationship with the overall tax system;
● suitability as a local tax;
● administration;
● the revenue/spending "mismatch";
● compatibility with possible constitutional reforms (in particular, territorial or regional government);
● the problems of transition to a new system.
We discuss each of these in turn.

Ability to pay

The theme running through this Report is that the tax system does not at present give proper attention to the relative abilities of different taxpayers to pay towards the provision of public services. The poll tax, even ameliorated by partial rebates, fails abjectly on this score. Rates, as they have been or in a reconstituted form based on capital values, score rather better, both because there is some link between people's incomes and because property itself is a legitimate component of an assessment of ability to pay. A tax based directly on income would score much better, providing one of the key arguments for a local income tax. At the same time, there is a limit on the extent to which it would be desirable for local taxation to perform a redistributive role. Too great a burden on those with the highest incomes could provoke the kind of "flight to the suburbs" phenomenon which has been much discussed in the United States, leaving behind inner cities with ever-dwindling tax bases. While we do not accept that this possibility implies that local taxation should be regressive, it does set a limit on how progressive it should be.

In the discussion below, we assume for this reason that a local income tax would take the form of a single tax rate for each authority charged on taxable income, and would not involve multiple rate bands. Moreover, it would be possible to set an upper limit to the amount of each taxpayer's taxable income on which a local income tax could be charged. Kay and Smith (1988) suggest that the top of the basic rate band would be appropriate. An analogous limit could be set within a graduated structure of tax rates, even if the basic rate band no longer existed. This kind of limitation would be in any case required if it was intended that local income tax rates should not add to the marginal rate of tax on the highest incomes.

One aspect of ability to pay which would be important in choosing how to run a local income tax depends on the dates at which income is received and tax is collected. If most tax is collected *at source* (as, for instance through the Pay As You Earn system (PAYE)), both happen at much the same time, and there is little problem. An alternative system, under which an assessment of income is made after the end of a tax year, and used as the tax base for a future year, could cause difficulties for those whose incomes had meanwhile fallen — for instance, because of unemployment, retirement, ill-health or child birth. A *rebate* system based on current income might be needed — which would both be very messy and lose some of the advantages of the income tax base.

In the case of capital value rates, the question arises as to whether the tax yield to be expected in different parts of the country should be in direct proportion to capital values — should local tax collections really be five times as high in London as in the North of England, given that the differential in incomes is not nearly so large? We can imagine four different responses:

(a) To say resolutely that the intention is to tax property as a legitimate part of the tax base, and that variations in property values should indeed be fully reflected in tax collections.

(b) To establish the grant system so that it *equalises* between different local authorities on the basis of relative *income* levels. Tax *rates* would then be lower in high value areas, so that collections would be similar. A problem with this occurs at the borders of areas with different incomes — two properties with equal values but on different sides of the border would attract different amounts of tax even if the authorities spent at the same level in relation to *need*. As a rather more approximate (but easier) measure, the *equalisation* could be done at a regional level. The same problem would arise at the regional borders, but this might be less

Chart 11.2: New rateable values and capital values

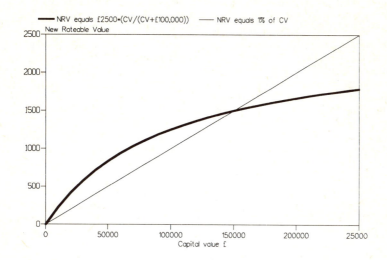

irksome. In recent years the *rate support grant* system has included a "London adjustment" of precisely this kind.

(c) To decide that the intended tax base was the "amenity" given by a particular property, rather than its actual value. Valuation could then be carried out on the basis of "standard" national prices for property with particular characteristics, excluding location. This would, however, lose the advantages of being able to use local property values as a reference point for valuation.

(d) To apply some kind of limit to taxable values. For instance, a simple cap could be put on the size of capital value which could count towards the tax base. Alternatively, it could be achieved by a formula such as that illustrated in Chart 11.2. A "new rateable value" would be calculated on the basis of capital value. For a house worth £150,000, it would be equal to one per cent of the capital value. For houses worth less than this amount it would be a larger percentage; for houses worth more, it would be a smaller percentage, giving some reassurance to those in high cost areas. The formula underlying the diagram is also shown, but for explanation to the general public a diagram or general principles would obviously be more suitable.

Relationship with the overall tax system

One of the merits of the rating system was that it filled what would otherwise have been a hole in the national system of taxation. In particular, domestic rates have acted as a tax on housing, offsetting some of the advantages which housing as a form of consumption or investment otherwise receives — housing in general benefitting through the lack of any other indirect tax on housing, and owner occupiers in particular through the combination of mortgage interest tax relief with exemption of capital gains and *imputed rents* from tax (see Chapter 7). With the abolition of domestic rates, housing will become still more tax-privileged (which would not be changed if the poll tax were replaced by a local income tax alone). It has been suggested that the abolition of rates may in the long run raise house prices by up to 15 per cent (Annex E of *Paying for Local Government*, Cmnd 9714, 1976). Other estimates have suggested that the effect could be even larger. The effects of this on consumer demand and the overall economy have prompted calls for a national property tax of some kind. The restoration of a local property tax can therefore be justified by the need to restore the balance which existed before.

The relationship between a local income tax and the national income tax deserves some attention. Many of the considerations which have shaped the national income tax (and our proposals for its reform) would apply equally to a local income tax. In particular, if equity considerations suggest one way of calculating taxable income for national purposes, we would expect them also to apply for a local income tax. This implies that the *taxable income* used to calculate local income tax should generally equal that used to calculate national income tax (which also eases administration). Similarly, the national income tax system has (for reasons discussed in Chapter 6) evolved to become a system of *individual* taxation, away from joint taxation of husband and wife. It would therefore be anomalous if local income tax was, for instance, assessed on any kind of joint basis, and we take it that a local income tax would be levied on a fully independent basis, as proposed for the national income tax.

Suitability as a source of local tax revenue

For a tax to be suitable for local use two basic requirements have to be met. The first is that the local tax base can be identified. The second is that it has to be possible for locally variable rates of tax to be charged.

We start with the question of identifying a local tax base. One of the reasons why the poll tax is so hard to collect and administer is that it is difficult to identify all potential taxpayers. There are particular problems for those who are highly mobile, students, those living in hostels, etc. Evasion is clearly an option which will be tried by those prepared to disappear from electoral rolls, library registers and so on. By contrast, a local income tax could start — as the national income tax does — with the much easier "tax handle" of the *sources* of income — such as employers, small businesses, banks and building societies. Because the people who are most difficult for administration of the poll tax are typically those with no or little income, they do not create such a collection problem for a tax on income. The problem which does arise is that of allocating income recipients to local authorities. This would require some kind of declaration of residence by income recipients to be used when tax came to be charged (it should be noted that one feature of the PAYE system is that the Inland Revenue does not necessarily have this information in an accurate form at present). It would also require a system to cope with people who move areas between financial years (or even within financial years if it was intended that a local income tax should be paid pro rata to residence). Identification of residence is clearly easier the wider the area covered, so that a regional income tax would have advantages in this respect. Finally, a property tax like rates presents little problem in the way of identifying the appropriate local authority.

The second basic requirement is local variability. There is no point in saying that a local tax system would support local decision-making if, in reality, there was no choice in the tax rate which could be set. This would be the case for a local sales tax, where a higher rate in, say, one London borough, would simply result in people switching their shopping to its lower tax neighbour. Tax rates would be bid down to the lowest level. Variability is not a great problem for a property tax like rates, as experience has shown. For a local income tax it depends on the system of administration (discussed further below). If the current *cumulative* PAYE system were retained, there would have to be limits on the number of local income tax rates which could be set — either through presenting authorities with a limited range of tax rates or through limiting the number of authorities which were involved (as would be the case with a regional income tax). This problem is obviously compounded if there are different tiers of authority — such as counties and districts — precepting on a local income tax: the decision of one tier could constrain the other even more tightly. If the national PAYE system were changed to one involving *universal end-year assessment*, these constraints on a local income tax would disappear.

Once these requirements are met, two linked issues arise: the *buoyancy* of the tax and its *perceptibility*. Rates — without annual property revaluations — were not a buoyant tax because the tax base stayed the same from year to year. The rate of tax (the *rate poundage* in this case) had to be raised each year just to keep up with rising prices and costs, even if authorities had not decided to provide any greater volume of services. This contrasts with the national income tax, where revenue automatically keeps up with overall incomes — indeed, it tends to run ahead, so that Chancellors can claim to be *cutting taxes* when they are in reality doing nothing of the kind. A local income tax would have similar properties of buoyancy. It has sometimes been suggested that the *lack* of buoyancy of taxes like rates is an advantage, requiring authorities to justify themselves to their voters every year, but this does not seem to us very convincing.

Linked to this, it is also argued that the way in which rates are collected — as a highly visible annual demand — is important as a way of ensuring local authority accountability. This would also be the case for a local income tax collected through a similar annual bill, but not for one collected, for instance, through the PAYE system. Whether this is a merit or a defect of a local income tax may depend on its purpose: as a sole *replacement* of the poll tax, a visible bill might be desirable; on the other hand, if a local income tax was *supplementing* a visible local tax like rates and effectively substituting for national income tax, an additional visible bill would give a misleading impression of what had happened to the tax burden.

A final issue is that of predictability of revenue. Local authorities work within a pretty well fixed annual budget, with limited scope for varying balances to cope with variations in income and spending from their original budgets. Rates provided a tax base which was largely fixed in advance and yielded a relatively predictable revenue. Again, the position with a local income tax depends on administration. If the tax was collected on the basis of a final assessment of taxable income in a previous year, the same predictable yield would be possible. If tax was collected at the same time as the income was generated (as with a PAYE-based system), the yield would be uncertain for two reasons. First, incomes may turn out to be higher or lower than the original forecast (on which the tax rates set would be based). Second, assuming that taxable income as established for national income tax was used, changes in a March Budget to personal tax allowances would affect the amount of income which was taxable. Such changes would come too late for local authority budgetting. Variability of revenue might be less of a problem for larger authorities, suggesting that an income tax is better suited to raise revenue for regional — rather than local — government.

Administration

The major administrative problem with capital value rates would be the establishment of the initial valuations and national house-by-house revaluations are quite expensive exercises, so they cannot happen every year (but see below). However, the longer between revaluations, the greater the relative shifts when they occur. Since the War the agony of this process has led governments to cancel revaluations to put off the evil day, only of course making the problem worse when it occurs (and leaving an unfair and out of date distribution of the tax burden in between). The potential effect of a rating revaluation in England and Wales (replacing the values last established in 1973), following the uncomfortable experience of the Scottish revaluation was one of the reasons why the poll tax has been introduced. If a new equivalent of rates was introduced, it would be essential to minimise the danger of this problem re-emerging. One possibility would be a system of *rolling revaluations*, with some of the properties in each region revalued each year, the whole country being covered, say, every five years. For the properties not physically revalued each year, a general uprating could be made on the basis of regional house price movements from sales records. This would keep valuations roughly in line with changing property values, with the five-yearly revaluations providing the fine tuning. Note that this would also result in a buoyant tax base, with the attendant advantages and disadvantages (although the buoyancy would be somewhat erratic, depending on short term fluctuations in house prices).

Administration issues are more important in the case of a local income tax. Here much of the debate revolves around whether it would be run through the current *cumulative* PAYE system for collecting national income tax, or whether that system would be changed to one involving *universal end-year assessment*. The overall issue of the choice between the two systems is discussed in Chapter 12. Essentially, a switch away from the cumulative system would have advantages in terms of removing administrative constraints on the income tax rate structure (allowing more and narrower tax bands), but would impose compliance costs on many taxpayers. It is for this reason that we do not favour abandoning the cumulative system, although we would favour a rather greater proportion of taxpayers receiving returns. We therefore discuss the local income tax on the assumption that the present cumulative system would be retained.

The current PAYE system imposes severe limits on how a local income tax could work. As total income assessments for a tax year simply do not exist for most taxpayers, a local income tax would have to be integrated with the national PAYE system. However, employers already have to cope with separate tax tables for each month or week of the year. These would have to be multiplied by the number of local tax rates to preserve the cumulative system with a local income tax collected at source. Large employers with computerised payrolls could cope relatively straightforwardly, but one only has to think of a small London employer trying to find the correct "Week 32" tables for each of the London boroughs in which employees live to realise that this could be a nightmare. There are two ways in which the number of tax rates could be cut down.

The first would be to restrict the choice of tax rate to, say, a range running in 0.5 per cent steps. This would create a severe "lumpiness" problem — authorities might only have the option of changing revenues by discrete steps. This virtually rules out a local income tax in this form as a sole revenue source (and would also rule out a combination of a local income tax in this form with a tax on another base where the two tax rates were tied together in fixed proportions, as this would not remove the "lumpiness"). Even with this restriction, the Inland Revenue has always maintained that it would still be impossible to allow areas as small as London boroughs to choose different tax rates under this system. The number of tax tables would not however be a problem for a regional or territorial income tax. There would then be "Scottish" or "South East England" tax tables and so on. Generally employers would find that nearly all of their employees lived within one region, so they would still be using one set of tables for most purposes.

A further restriction imposed by trying to run a local income tax without end-year assessments would be that investment income would have to be taxed at a fixed national rate (mainly through an addition to the *composite* rate and an adjustment to the imputation system for dividends). This would mean that the local income tax base would not be *comprehensive* in the way we have been proposing for national income tax. On the other hand, it would remove the incentive for those with large investment incomes to move to (or use a correspondence address in) "local tax havens".

The revenue/spending "mismatch"

Taken together, Table 11.1 and Chart 11.1 illustrate a central issue in local authority finance. Most of what local government does involves the provision of services of national importance, often with national controls over standards, rather than with purely local benefits and with local discretion over standards. In recognition of this, much of its spending is financed by grants from central government (albeit significantly less than used to be the case). But this means that the sources of revenue over which local authorities have control only account for a small part of their budgets. In its 1976 report the Layfield Committee on Local Government Finance argued that this "mismatch" caused problems of accountability — those doing the spending did not bear the responsibility for raising the revenue. It suggested there were two routes which could be taken to remove them — a "centralist" option, with central government assuming more direct responsibility and control over the spending which it paid for, and a "localist" option, which would enhance the local tax base, specifically through *addition* of a local income tax to revenue from rates.

In the event, there has been a move towards more central control, and the local tax base will become even narrower with the nationalisation of non-domestic rates from April 1990. The only discretionary source of income for local authorities in Great Britain will then be the poll tax, only accounting for a quarter or less of local spending. With revenue from central government grant and shares from the national non-domestic rate fixed whatever an authority spends, the phenomenon of "gearing" will be intensified. For example, an authority may decide to spend 10 per cent more than the amount set by central government as necessary to produce a "standard" level of services. Since it pays for only a small proportion of standard spending, the consequent increase in poll tax would be much higher, perhaps 40 per cent, arguably giving a false impression of relative efficiency.

Gearing could be (and in the past was) reduced through the structure of the grant system. Even so, it is not necessarily healthy that the narrowness of local government's tax base makes the grant system — which has increased in complexity and general incomprehensibility as rapidly as the Department of the Environment's computing capacity has allowed — of such critical importance. It might not matter if there were agreed and objective ways of assessing what a "standard" level of service would consist of and how much it would cost each authority to provide. In reality, grant determination involves a great deal of political judgement, favouritism and haggling. The narrow tax base makes this worse.

Accompanying any change to local taxation a position therefore has to be taken on two issues:

- should all the spending which is at present made by local government continue to be so?
- what proportion of this taxation should be financed through local taxation?

In response to the first of these questions it can be argued that, for instance, teachers' pay makes up a large proportion of local spending, but involves very little in the way of local discretion, being the result of national negotiations. Making items like this part of central government's budget would substantially reduce Layfield's "mismatch" problem. On the other hand, while the *rates* of pay may be set nationally, the mix of education spending between, say, staff and equipment is something that is decided locally — to some extent, indeed, at school level. "Centralising" only one part of the education budget would make this kind of local budgetting more difficult.

The answer to this question will also depend on the extent and responsibility of regional or territorial government: one answer to the "mismatch" would be to inject new elements of *accountability* through regional assemblies. This would imply devolution of part of the responsibility — and cost — of central grants to the regions, depending on whether this was thought to be an appropriate part of their functions.

Constitutional change

The final report of the Labour Party's Policy Review, *Meet the Challenge, Make the Change*, proposes that a Scottish Assembly be established with powers to vary income tax rates, that there also be a Welsh Assembly, and perhaps ten regional assemblies in England. Local taxation therefore has to be seen in terms of its relationship to regional as well as national taxation. As well as having advantages in terms of democracy and political pluralism, the creation of Scottish, Welsh and English regional assemblies would inject a new element into the relationship between accountability, revenue-raising and spending. For instance, instead of most of the revenue for public spending (local and central) in Scotland coming from a central government allocation over which Scottish voters have no control, the Scottish Assembly would be able to impose Scottish preferences on the way in which that money was spent. Power to vary income tax rates would, in effect, mean that there was a Scottish income tax rate (or precept), substituting for part of the national income tax rate.

Clearly it would be sensible to avoid duplication of tax collection. This implies either that different tiers have their own tax bases, or, if they share a tax base, that a single collection system is used, with a system of *precepts* building up a combined tax rate (as is done in establishing total rate poundages — or poll tax rates — from the different tiers of local authorities at present — such as district and county councils). However, particular bases are more suitable for collection at different levels — property is in many ways the easiest tax base to assign to authorities covering relatively small areas, while income may be more suitable as a base for larger areas, like regions. Provided that the system of grants from central government functions properly, we do not think that the assignment of different bases to different tiers should be ruled out on the grounds that each tier should have a base with identical features in terms of aspects like buoyancy or visibility.

Problems of transition

As mentioned at the start of this chapter, it seems inevitable that there will be two separate phases to the replacement of the poll tax. There will have to be immediate moves to reduce some of its worst effects (for instance, by extending rebates to cover up to 100 per cent of the tax for those with the lowest incomes), but a permanent replacement local tax will take some time — probably several years — to establish. The fact that there will thus be two points of change immediately brings out the need for co-ordination. Without co-ordination it is perfectly possible to end up antagonising those adversely affected by one of its two stages, even though they benefitted overall. Anyone who doubts the problems this can cause has only to look at the row within the Conservative Party in 1989 over *safety nets* for English and Welsh local authorities during the introduction of the poll tax and associated changes. Essentially, the changes have two separate kinds of distributional effect — one relating to the substitution of the poll tax for domestic rates, the other to the position of local authorities under the new grant and national non-domestic rate arrangements. People losing on the swings of the first may make a larger gain on the roundabouts of the second. Overall, they would be *gainers* from the change. However, the Government decided to phase in the second set of effects (so as to prevent the position of those losing on the swings *and* the roundabouts showing up too soon). This turns some *overall* gainers into losers at the moment the poll tax is introduced. The Government has now said that the gains on the roundabouts will come in full before the next election (although losses will still be delayed).

This problem has two implications. First, it would be politically unwise to be so generous in any immediate change that the eventual reform — seen by itself — looked unfavourable by comparison with, say, a massively rebated poll tax. The second is that there is a premium on getting the second change to happen as soon as possible after the first, so that memories of the original position, the pre-election poll tax, have not faded. However, the last ten years are littered with examples of central government imposing changes on local government with too short a timetable for proper administration, not least the poll tax itself. The options for replacing the poll tax will all take time — restoration of a rating system but based on capital values would require a valuation exercise for the whole country. The 1973 domestic rating revaluation took 4 years. An interim system based on old rateable values could be restored quickly (if authorities had not destroyed their rating rolls), but would introduce another point of change and would probably make the final phase of the transition — to capital value rates — less attractive. Whether this would be worthwhile would depend on how long the full valuation was going to take: if it was several years, we would favour an interim system based on old rateable values.

A regional tax of any kind would require regional assemblies to be established, elected and to make their own decisions on tax rates, a process which would take most of the life of a parliament (especially if it involved constitutional legislation).

If some *combination* of options were to be used, there would be a choice between introducing all the changes together, with the pace being set by the slowest, or bringing them in separately — creating further stages to the transition and added potential for *losers* to be created at one stage out of *overall* gainers.

Local taxes on business

Most of this chapter is concerned with local domestic taxes. However, it should be noted that a further narrowing of the local tax base is occurring as a result of the nationalisation of non-domestic rates. Restoration of locally variable non-domestic rates could reverse this. However, it should be noted that if the grant equalisation system fully adjusts for differences between authorities in their non-domestic rate bases — which the *block grant* since 1980 did, except in the case of a few unusually wealthy authorities — then it makes no difference to the authority or its domestic taxpayers how much non-domestic rateable value there is. The main effect of locally variable non-domestic rates between 1980 and 1989 was to penalise businesses in the areas which the Government designated as "high spenders" liable to grant penalties, without any effect on individual local authorities' finances. Further, with few exceptions, authorities have not "benefitted" from the promotion of local businesses in recent years in the way they once did from the expansion it allowed of their tax bases. In fact, the reverse is the case if allowances for what will now be called *standard spending* fail to allow for the costs which local employers impose on local authority services.

While it would be wrong to establish a grant system which left authorities in areas without much in the way of business at a great disadvantage, it would seem desirable that local government should have some stake in the development of business in its area. There are two ways in which this could be done. First, non-domestic rates could be returned to being a local tax, but with the grant system set up so that it did not fully equalise for variations in non-domestic rateable value between authorities. This would, of course, mean that some areas would be somewhat better resourced than others. If this is unacceptable, it implies that non-domestic rates should stay nationalised. One way of lessening the conflict between aims could be to equalise on the basis of, say, existing non-domestic properties, but to leave future developments generating net additions to local resources.

A second measure could be to copy what is done in Paris, where a levy on employers' wage bills contributes to funding the transport network in the region. A "London" addition to employer National Insurance contributions could both produce revenue to cope with the capital's critical transport needs and would act as a tax on congestion which might have some effect on encouraging more balanced economic growth.

Conclusions

Three factors appear to be of particular importance. The first is the problem of the timing of the introduction of a replacement to the poll tax which we have just discussed. Second are the administrative problems which face a local income tax as a single source of revenue, given the view that the present cumulative PAYE system be retained. Thirdly, a key role would be played by decisions about "centralising" of part of local spending or increasing the proportion of local spending paid for by grant.

Our preference for the eventual system is for a capital value rate, to be accompanied by a regional income tax if constitutional changes are made to introduce regional assemblies. We believe that the administrative, and other, problems of a local income tax rule out its playing a major role at the local (as opposed to regional) level.

The introduction of a capital value rate (and possible regional income tax) will take a considerable time. We recommend that in the meantime 100 per cent rebates be introduced for the poll tax, easing the burden on those with lowest incomes, but that the tax otherwise be left unchanged. Finally, we recommend that — if the burden on local finance is to be reduced — this should accompany the introduction of the capital value rate.

Chapter 12

Administration and enforcement

This report is about the structure of direct taxation and the ways in which it could and should be reformed to make it more equitable. In framing the recommendations in previous chapters we have, however, been careful to pay attention to the constraints which the practicalities of administration place on reform. In this chapter we discuss some of the key issues involved, including the general approach to administration and promoting compliance.

Administrative constraints on reform

Administrative constraints have often been exaggerated in the past, with reform proposals met with the response that "they might well be desirable in principle, but the administrative problems of introducing them would, sadly, prove insuperable...". We are sceptical about this general response for two reasons.

First, a glance at the tax systems of other countries shows that there are many other ways of structuring an income tax system from that which has evolved in Britain and that taxpayers and tax administrations cope with them with much the same level of compliance and grumbling as here. To take a key example, Britain is different from most other OECD countries in its structure of income tax where virtually all taxpayers are liable at the same, basic, marginal rate. If it is argued that to change this, as we have suggested, to give wider variation of rates would be administratively impossible, then this objection can be met with a list of all the other OECD countries which cope with this "impossibility".

Second, for many years reformers were told that their proposals might be desirable in principle, but unfortunately the computerisation of the Inland Revenue would have to be finished before implementation could be considered. This rather lengthy process has now been completed, and the computer systems installed have considerably more flexibility than is currently exploited. As the Inland Revenue's then Assistant Director of Data Processing put it to the Sub-committee of the House of Commons Treasury and Civil Service Committee, the system is designed "to cope with changes in rate, lower rates or higher rates, wider or shorter rate bands, and broadly speaking, the tax rates built into the computer system are parameterised so that a change simply involves changing the parameters" (HC 20-I, 1982-83, Q.1061).

Income tax collection

The bulk of income tax and employee National Insurance contributions is collected through the Pay As You Earn (PAYE) system by employers. Only a small proportion of tax on employment income is collected through the completion of a tax return at the end of the tax year, followed by Inland Revenue assessment of the tax due; although for the self-employed tax is collected through submission of accounts after the year end. Most tax on investment income (interest from banks and building societies and company dividends) is also collected at source, with only relatively small amounts collected through the tax return and assessment system. Capital gains tax is collected by using a separate section of the annual income tax return, but inheritance tax is administered separately.

The income tax system has two particular features which allow much of the tax to be collected at source, reducing the amount of work which has to be carried out by the Inland Revenue. First, there is the nature of the PAYE system. Income tax on employment incomes in Britain (and in Ireland, but nowhere else) is collected through a self-adjusting cumulative PAYE system. This works so that by the end of the year most employees will have paid the correct amount of tax on their total income for the year (including any other regular income sources which have been allowed for in their PAYE *coding*). The work is done by employers, who use tax tables or computerised payroll programs to calculate the tax to be deducted each week or month. This is based not just on income during that period and one week or month's worth of tax allowances, but allowing for total income received in the year so far and for total tax charged in the year so far.

This system means that for the majority of earners the correct amount of tax is deducted by the end of the year without any need for an "end-year correction" — a tax refund or a further tax bill — as required in many other countries. Where extra tax is found to be due at the end of the year, it is often collected through an adjustment to PAYE payments in the following year.

The second feature is that much tax on investment income is deducted at source — by the bank or building society paying interest or the company paying dividends — at a fixed rate. This is deemed (through the composite rate system for interest or through the imputation system for dividends) to cover the tax due from basic rate taxpayers.

Given that the majority of taxpayers are liable to tax at the basic rate, the combination of these two features means that the correct amount of tax is deducted without any direct contact between the taxpayer and the Inland Revenue. Less than a fifth of employees have to complete a tax return giving full details of their income and allowances claimed. These are necessary for those liable (or possibly liable) to the higher rate and who might therefore be due to pay additional tax on investment income taxed at source or able to claim allowances like mortgage interest relief against the higher rate. They are also necessary for those who may have sources of income, such as income from self-employment, rents, capital gains, or casual earnings and for those who want to claim special allowances. Some allowances — for instance, claims for the married man's or married couple's allowance or regular work expenses — can be dealt with through the PAYE *coding* sent to employers at the start of the year, which enables employer deductions to take account of them.

This system clearly has advantages for the Inland Revenue and saves most employees from the labours which end-year assessments place on taxpayers in other countries. However, it imposes major administrative costs on employers, particularly those which are not computerised. They have to use different tax tables for each period to calculate tax due on the basis of income so far during the tax year. It also creates the need for information on income tax paid in one employment to be passed on to the next employer (via "P45" forms), and for the Inland Revenue to keep track of this *movements* operation.

The system has collection benefits compared with one in which small amounts of underpaid tax might have to be collected after the year end from large numbers of taxpayers. However it seems that there are compliance costs from the low level of contact between taxpayers and the Inland Revenue. We note in particular that the Keith Committee recommended that it would be desirable for a wider range of taxpayers to be sent tax returns, as the arrival of the form often prompts reporting of income which would otherwise escape the system. Most people are prepared to pay the tax due from them when it is requested, but they do not necessarily do so unprompted. While this may not justify the sending of a tax return to all taxpayers, it does mean that some widening of the range of taxpayers to whom they are sent would generate additional revenue to defray the administrative costs involved.

The facts that most employees do not receive tax returns and that no assessment of their total income for the year is ever made raises particular problems for the introduction of a local income tax (see Chapter 11). So does the fact that the Inland Revenue does not at present have to worry particularly about the accuracy of the addresses for taxpayers on its files (mostly sent in by employers): they are often not very important for running the system, and tax liability does not depend on where people live within the country (so there is no reason for anyone not to be truthful).

The alternative would be to come into line with the rest of the world by switching to a system of approximate deductions (based only on that period's income) and end-year assessments of income and adjustments of tax due. This would lessen the compliance burden on employers, but increase it on individual taxpayers, who might not welcome the unfamiliar prospect of filling in annual tax returns. The Inland Revenue would have to cope with returns and assessments for all taxpayers, but could abandon its *movements* operation linking tax paid in different employments.

Universal end-year assessment would make it easier to make changes like abandoning the long basic rate income tax band, ending the inequities caused by the *composite rate* system for taxing investment income at source, or introducing a local income tax. While overseas experience is that this kind of system can work smoothly, the transition to it in Britain might well be unpopular through the substantial increase it would imply for the compliance burden on ordinary taxpayers. Many might find themselves unable to understand the system without incurring the costs of employing "tax return compilers", and it would tend to be the least well off who ended up failing to claim back any over-paid tax. Such systems work best if there is a general bias towards overpayment of tax during the year and refunds at the year end, but this means that some people would have to manage on lower net incomes during the year before the final adjustment was made.

On balance we believe that, if it is possible, the cumulative system should be maintained, avoiding universal tax returns and end-year assessment. This raises questions connected with our recommendations for the income tax rate structure, to which we now turn.

Graduation and tax administration

It is sometimes supposed that avoiding universal end-year assessment requires the existence of the long basic rate of income tax and that a move to graduation would inevitably mean that Britain would have to move to this system. Graduation by itself does not, however, require this. This can be seen by looking in turn at the different sources of income:

(a) Income from **employment**. This is taxed through the PAYE system. Given that this is done through using tables giving tax due from certain income levels in particular weeks of the tax year or through payroll computer programs, the difficulties in moving to a system with a wider variety of tax rates are minimal. The West German system has incorporated a complicated algebraic formula for determining tax liability without it causing any problems for this part of the system. Indeed, the British system has coped with a much more varied rate structure in the past. In the minority of cases where there are tax returns and the Inland Revenue has to combine income from different sources at the end of the year to calculate an assessment of liability, the computer programs now used by the Revenue could cope with a more complicated structure.

(b) Income from **self-employment, rents, capital gains, etc.** These are taxed through submission of accounts and assessments after the end of the tax year. Again, Inland Revenue computerised assessment programs can cope with a much more complicated tax structure than we now have.

(c) **Investment income taxed at source.** This is the area where a move to graduation might require an increase in the number of tax returns. If more people were subject to a wider variety of marginal tax rates, it would be less likely that tax collected at a flat rate at source would turn out to be correct. In these cases further adjustment might be needed.

It is therefore only for this last source of income that major problems arise.

There are two ways in which they could be moderated, however, if it was desired to continue to avoid tax returns and assessments for the majority of taxpayers. First, even with a structure involving many different rate bands, the need for widespread use of tax returns could still be avoided if the *composite rate* system was continued. However, as we have discussed in Chapter 7, this system involves a degree of "rough justice" in that the tax deducted is an average of the tax which would be due from those liable at the basic rate (including the basic rate part of higher rate tax) and from non-taxpayers. The latter cannot reclaim this tax. The same system could be used to deduct tax at a fixed rate, exempting from tax liability at several of the tax rates at the bottom of a structure with narrow steps. This could cover as great a proportion of taxpayers as was required. This would be a compromise, but it would still allow the benefits of a narrowly stepped structure — if this was desired — to apply to all other sources of income, without the taxation of interest receipts ruling it out. It should be noted that dividend income is taxed under separate rules where adjustment is made to the taxpayer's actual marginal tax rate, so that a wider variety of tax rates would increase the number of adjustments needed. This, however affects many fewer people than interest income.

We do not, however, find the "rough justice" implied by the composite rate system as it is now acceptable. It results in non-taxpayers subsidising those with higher incomes if they save through the most readily available channels like banks and building societies. We see a great advantage in maintaining a *withholding* system of taxation on the bulk of investment income, but believe that non-taxpayers should be allowed to reclaim tax withheld, as they already can for dividends.

Our preferred option is therefore that the structure of graduated tax bands should be designed in such a way that, while no longer having a single band for 95 per cent of taxpayers, it retains a fairly wide initial band. If tax is withheld at source at this rate on investment income, many taxpayers would still pay the correct amount of tax automatically. Those not liable for tax would have to file a return in order to reclaim the withheld tax, but this situation appears preferable to the present one with the composite rate where they cannot claim a refund. Those above the initial band would have to pay additional tax, but, as we have said above, a rather wider distribution of tax returns to those with incomes above this level could well be desirable in itself for the reasons discussed by the Keith Committee, and should not be seen as a drawback of graduation.

Simplification of tax administration

A move towards graduation does therefore involve some increase in the activity of the Inland Revenue as would some of our proposals for widening the tax base and for changing the composite rate system into a withholding tax. These changes are justified on equity grounds, despite some administrative costs.

For many of our other recommendations, however, our proposals would not only make the tax system fairer but would also greatly simplify tax assessment and would liberate administrative resources:

- fully independent taxation would put a complete end to the need to link the tax records of husbands and wives;
- restricting reliefs like mortgage interest relief to a single rate would mean that the current complications of calculating higher rate relief would disappear;
- the abolition of special allowances and deductions like Personal Equity Plans, private health insurance relief, concessions for share option schemes or the Business Expansion Scheme would remove them from the tax calculation;
- the ending of the National Insurance ceiling and of income tax deductibility of Class 4 NICs would also simplify administration.

Avoidance and evasion

The "tax industry" is itself big business and each year the publicity machines of the major accounting firms boast ever increasing revenues from the provision of taxation services. We recognise that some of these services are compliance related and that without the availability of such services the task of the Inland Revenue and Customs and Excise would be made much more difficult. Whatever changes we propose to the tax system — and we would argue that overall these would constitute a simplification — it will remain complex and in parts highly technical.

However, there is a considerable loss to the Exchequer for a variety of reasons ranging from the failure to report small scale earnings (such as tips) to sophisticated international "planning" devices. Some of this loss is illegal although some, however morally reprehensible, is perfectly legal.

We do not argue that we expect everyone to organise their affairs so as to pay as much tax as possible and thus forego reliefs and exemptions deliberately provided for within the system. However, we do recognise that because there will always be rules which circumscribe a tax regime, there will always be efforts to "plan" around these rules.

Even if there were no reliefs in a taxation system, the requirement to have national tax boundaries, the fact that tax is collected for a time period (a tax year) and a graduated rate structure, means that planning will be undertaken.

Our objective is to reinforce compliance procedures so as to minimise the risk of evasion and to construct the rules of our system in such a way that unacceptable planning is made as difficult as possible. Avoidance and evasion come in a variety of forms, which we now discuss.

International operations of transnational groups

Here, the opportunities for tax planning are probably at their greatest. Such opportunities exist because of the power and flexibility that transnationals have in locating operations in many territories. The operations need not necessarily entail a substantial physical presence in any particular territory. Avoidance includes the use of tax havens or other low tax territories for financial transactions. "Transfer-Pricing" involves groups of companies pricing transactions within the group but between territories to achieve the best overall tax position for the group. This does not necessarily mean that profits will always be put into low tax territories because the history of the group could involve say, a UK company which had other losses which were available for offset.

Such groups have a great deal of flexibility as to whether they operate in any territory as a branch or as a subsidiary and whether they capitalise subsidiaries by way of share capital or by debt. The latter is particularly important because it determines where the interest deductions can be made. Indeed, for a long period of time before recent anti-avoidance legislation so-called "link companies" enabled tax deductions to be taken in two territories for the same interest payments!

With related matters like interest flows or royalty flows, there is the ability to use double taxation treaties, which are agreements, usually bilateral, between two territories allowing for say a reduced rate of withholding tax or royalty payments from one to the other.

Schemes

These might be planned on a domestic or an international basis; they might be marketed widely or "tailor-made"; they may be extremely complex or quite straightforward. One might characterise them as using legislation to achieve a tax consequence which is inconsistent with the spirit or intention of that legislation. They might be taken up in conjunction with the attainment of some commercial objective — the sale of a company or, more generally for example, the use of discretionary trusts — as part of the corporate or individual's environment.

Employment earnings

Tax evasion on employment earnings which are not subject to PAYE and which the individual (or employer) does not separately report to the Inland Revenue may be less sophisticated but nevertheless, requires our attention. The individual involved may not have properly declared relevant details to the employer — incorrect name or income details of other employment — or the employer may fail to apply the appropriate rules. Such failures may be deliberate or simply errors; they may be isolated or part of a general plan, particularly on the part of the employers. The employer in such cases might be a person who is conducting a business and, therefore, generally seeking tax deductions for employment expenses or an individual who would not be able to claim a tax deduction for the expenses — for example, someone employing a housekeeper. Generally such transactions would be in cash and often the employment would be part-time and/or short term.

We should note that our concern extends not only to tax, but also to the fact that such employment arrangements could deny the individual recourse to employment rights, and to rights under the social security benefits which accrue by virtue of a contribution record. Where second employments are concerned, the individual might not be losing much, but for someone's sole employment the loss of rights is clearly disastrous. Indeed this touches on a wider issue where we need to safeguard not only the proper collection of revenue but also the implementation of, for example, minimum pay legislation.

Non-compliance by businesses

This heading also covers a variety of possibilities. At its simplest, it could involve the extraction and underpayment of cash takings from a till. It might involve no reporting at all — particularly for casual cash businesses (window cleaning, car repairing). The evasion may not only involve income tax or corporation tax, it could also involve the under-reporting of VAT.

This type of evasion can be undertaken without the collusion of others because the persons supplying the revenues are, generally, individual consumers who would not, themselves be seeking a tax deduction for their expenditure. However, even if such a tax deduction was sought, it would be impossible to trace the item to verify that the receipt had been properly accounted for by the supplier.

At a more sophisticated level, there could be collusion between two parties. For example, an overseas supplier of goods might be persuaded to inflate the price of these goods to a UK purchaser and channel a "discount" into an offshore bank account, which goes unreported. Such evasion is, of course, assisted by bank secrecy laws. More mundane would be attempts to "live off the company", channelling as much personal expenditure as possible through the business.

A further aspect of non-compliance concerns the manner in which annual taxation computations are prepared and submitted to the Inland Revenue for their agreement. Submissions may misclassify items so as to give a tax advantage, or perhaps more commonly, may take the benefit of the doubt on the tax deductibility of an item. In this latter case, because only small numbers of cases are examined in detail, the issue is never properly examined. To demonstrate the scale of this the 129th *Report of the Board of the Inland Revenue* (for the period to 31 March 1987), indicated that "Technical Work" generated adjustments to tax returns and accounted for additional revenues of approximately £1 billion in each of 1985/6 and 1986/7. Whilst it may not be correct to suggest that this is just the tip of the iceberg, the percentage of accounts which are examined in depth — 2.2 per cent — suggests that a lot more revenue is at stake.

At its crudest, tax evasions can involve the fraudulent extraction of monies from companies so that there are no resources to pay tax which is properly due. Businesses, of course, are not only taxpayers because they generate profits. They act as collecting agents for the Inland Revenue, Department of Social Security and Customs and Excise and failure to fulfil these duties, particularly in relation to VAT can give rise to substantial revenue losses, while failure to remit National Insurance contributions can result in employees losing entitlement to pensions and other benefits.

Non-compliance by individuals

We have previously touched upon non-compliance in relation to employment income, but non-compliance involves failure to report investment income and capital gains. For investment income, failure to report will lead to a loss of revenue where such income is not covered by the tax credit or composite rate arrangements or higher rate tax is due. Further, the ability to trace such income is difficult where overseas income may be involved (which is not collected through a UK paying agent), particularly where bearer securities are the source of such income.

Non-compliance for individuals is not just a matter of not reporting income, gains or gifts, but can involve misrepresentation of residence status. Currently, residence is generally determined by reference to physical presence in the UK, and in some circumstances, by "available accommodation", although proposals have been floated for determination purely on grounds of presence in the UK for a certain number of days in a tax year. In practice some individuals have been able to misleadingly represent a non-resident status, particularly helped by such locations as the Channel Islands.

In a similar vein, some trusts which are effectively under the control of UK resident and domiciled individuals present a facade of offshore status, perpetuated by side letters and lack of honesty on the part of some professional advisers.

Tackling avoidance and evasion

It should be clear that the nature and extent of tax avoidance and evasion means that there is no single solution which will achieve an objective. We highlight the following as our recommended strategy:

Increased resources for the Inland Revenue and Customs and Excise

One clear area of policy in tackling avoidance and evasion is to inject more resources into the Inland Revenue and Customs and Excise. If scrutiny of some 2 per cent of business accounts can generate adjustments producing £1 billion per year, then improving that figure to just 5 per cent is likely to generate significant additional revenue.

It is clear that improvements in the morale of tax collecting staff and in retention rates are a high priority. While it may not be possible to match salaries in the most lucrative parts of the private sector, it is clearly a false economy to hold down salaries to such a level that the revenue departments simply act as a training school for tax advisers.

Resources for the Inland Revenue and Customs and Excise must not only be about personnel but about equipment. We should generally support the moves towards greater use of computers as this will, *inter alia*, allow greater sophistication in analysing and identifying returns and accounts which, *prima facie*, require greater scrutiny.

Control procedures of the Inland Revenue and Customs and Excise
An extensive review of the possibilities is outside the scope of this Report. However, we would urge consideration of two matters in particular.

The first of these is for there to be greater emphasis and co-ordination on control visits encompassing more liaison with the Department of Social Security and whatever bodies might be involved in the enforcement of minimum wage legislation. The second is the introduction of a *general Revenue audit*. At present, apart from the control visits referred to above and rather specialised situations — for example, the involvement of Enquiry Branch — there is no general visit to business premises to inspect accounting records and supporting documentation. Such in-depth reviews as are undertaken of business accounts generally proceed by correspondence between the Inspector of Taxes and the taxpayer's agent. This generally puts the taxpayer at an advantage, as carefully controlled correspondence can often serve to accentuate the positive aspects of a case and to downplay difficult features.

Enforcement powers of revenue departments
In December 1986, the Board of the Inland Revenue published a consultative document on the recommendation of the Keith Committee on income tax, capital gains tax and corporation tax. The consultative document comments in paragraph 1.2.1:

> *"Keith sought in the report to put together a balanced package of recommendations. It accepted that the Revenue Departments should have sufficient powers to encourage people to honour their tax liabilities at the right time, and to ensure that a small minority could not, by delay or outright evasion, count on gaining an unfair advantage over taxpayers generally. But Keith considered that those powers should be exercised within a framework which ensured that individual taxpayers were sufficiently protected against any undue or unnecessary intrusion into personal privacy, and generally against any abuse of powers. For this purpose, it recommended that the Revenue Departments' use of their powers should be controlled within clear statutory rules, defining the rights as well as the obligations of taxpayers, incorporating clear rights of appeal and subject always to judicial supervision by the independent Appeal Commissioners (Special and General) and the courts."*

The thrust of these proposals is something we very much support. Similarly, the proposals relating to Customs and Excise have our support. Some of the Keith Committee proposals have already been adopted and others are in the pipeline. It is suggested that some which have been rejected we would wish to reinstate. Reference has already been made to general powers of entry to inspect business records. Furthermore, Keith's Recommendation 30 relating to the taking of the benefit of the doubt, would have a powerful effect on the collection of revenue, and should be taken up.

Regulation of tax advisers

To act as an agent for a taxpayer, no particular qualification is needed; even where there is a professional qualification, standards are by no means universal. Standards vary on technical competence as well as on matters of integrity. It is known that the Inland Revenue makes its own internal assessment of accountancy firms. This leads us to ask why, just as we have regulation of those operating in the financial services sector, and, *inter alia*, trade unions, could we not have a register of those authorised to provide taxation services within the UK? The register could be reinforced by refusing deductibility for fees paid to non-registered individuals. Persons wishing to avail themselves of a registered provider of taxation services could consult the public register. Consideration would have to be given to who was to compile and be the guardian of the register, and we believe that this should be undertaken by an organisation independent of the Inland Revenue and Customs and Excise. Entry on the register would, obviously be denied to those who were involved in fraud, but to also those for whom, over a period of time, it could be demonstrated had not generally complied with guidelines of say "reasonable disclosure".

We would recognise that in handling compliance matters and assisting the interpretation of complex legislation, tax advisers have a role to play in enhancing the process of Revenue gathering. Thus, to create a regime for them which was unduly harsh and unrelenting would not be in the best interest of the Inland Revenue or Customs and Excise. However, there is a strong case for providing an incentive for improved standards.

Such registration could not, of course, cover those who submitted business or individual returns under their own name, or groups of companies which had their own in-house arrangements. In the latter case, however, obligations on the chief executive would provide the necessary discipline. We could also enhance standards by requiring professional advisers who compiled returns and acted as agents to have also to sign such returns and to be liable for penalties for failure to apply due diligence. This is broadly the position for returns submitted to the US Internal Revenue Service.

The role of auditors of companies is commonly misunderstood and their current role is broadly one of determining whether accounts show a true and fair view. This is not the same as verifying all of the transactions in a set of accounts or confirming that fraud is absent. Nevertheless, a competent audit should point out weaknesses in internal controls and may uncover irregularities. So far as taxation matters are concerned, we could, in theory, place auditors under a separate obligation to "sign off" to the effect that there were no taxation irregularities, but it is difficult to see that this is a practical proposition. However, there is a *prima facie* case for requiring the auditor when it comes within his knowledge to "blow the whistle" to the revenue authorities on cases of fraud. Auditing guidelines permit direct discussion with the Bank of England in relation to banking irregularities, and providing clear guidelines are given, such a procedure must assist the proper process of revenue gathering.

Legislation and regulations

Our clear approach to tax avoidance is to have specific legislation to counteract abuse of the system. Such legislation might be enhanced by detailed regulations. There is a range of topics which can be clearly identified and some merit separate discussion in their own right. Legislation and case law may currently exist for some of the items but are inadequate. By way of illustration, one may identify:

(a) Transfer pricing — the existing general anti-avoidance provision is inadequate. It would be possible to specify much more precisely the guidelines which should be adopted, and require responsible officials of taxpayer companies and/or auditors to confirm compliance.

(b) Debt/equity — much more specific guidelines exist in the USA concerning the extent to which a company can be capitalised by debt and a tax deduction for the interest obtained.

(c) Employment versus self-employment — current distinctions based on case law could be tightened to reduce the benefit of the latter classification.

(d) Controlled foreign companies — the UK regime which seeks to reach tax haven operations of UK controlled companies is much weaker than its US counterpart.

(e) Trusts — the tax regime surrounding trusts is highly complex and is extensively used for avoiding personal income tax, capital gains tax and, of course, inheritance tax. Discretionary trusts, in particular, are a major tool of the tax avoider.

As indicated above, the foregoing is illustrative and certainly not definitive. However, we emphasise that a Labour Government should have a substantial legislative programme on these issues alone quite apart from more fundamental tax changes it would introduce. The time commitment and the process of this has to be carefully thought through. Certainly, the concept of a Tax Reform Act, quite separate from the annual Finance Act, has its attractions.

However, we should recognise that, no matter how rigorous and specifically targetted legislation will be, there will remain scope for avoidance and we need to reflect on how this can be tackled. First the courts could be encouraged to depart from what was, prior to the "Ramsay" and "Furniss v Dawson" decisions, a somewhat traditional narrower construction of taxing statutes. This so-called "new approach" was commented on in a report by the Special Committee of Tax Law Consultative Bodies. It criticised the approach for creating uncertainty and failure to identify the principles for determining the basis upon which, and for what purpose, transactions are, or are not, to be regarded as having taken place. For our part, we also recognise that such an approach can create uncertainty for businesses for "genuine" transactions.

Second, there could be a general anti-avoidance provision. The Law Society has set its face against this approach and favours clearly targetted legislation. Nevertheless, there are existing precedents for example, Australia, New Zealand and a recent anti-avoidance provision in Canada. It is argued that such general anti-avoidance provisions inevitably involve the courts in interpretations on what should be matters for Parliament. Whilst this is accepted, at least the framework of the anti-avoidance provision is provided by Parliament, and not invented as in the current "new approach". On the issue of uncertainty that it might create, this could be catered for by advance rulings. These currently exist, for example, in relation to capital gains tax on share for share transactions and, generally, for transactions in securities.

International co-operation
It is clear from an OECD Report on avoidance and evasion (OECD (1987)) that enhancements in combatting tax avoidance can be achieved through further international co-operation. This can be encompassed within OECD treaties on a multi-lateral basis or in strengthening arrangements on a bi-lateral basis. The co-operation should extend to more extensive exchange of information, joint investigations of particular taxpayers, and joint efforts in reviewing tax havens.

Individual pressure
Part of our process should be to give individuals sufficient incentive and protection so that for some types of evasion they are unwilling to be involved. For example, by ensuring that individuals have protection on minimum pay levels, opportunity to engage in trade union activity, rights to pursue at the workplace, they are less likely to be subdued into accepting status as non-employees.

Other mechanisms
Combatting tax avoidance can also be assisted by an all-embracing and specifically targetted approach on some tax havens. This is a technique adopted by the US to some extent in respect of the Caribbean basin.

For example, in relation to the Channel Islands, the UK Government could bring to bear pressures on a number of fronts to encourage changes in the tax and financial regime which allows the UK tax to be avoided. In particular, the matter of bank secrecy laws could be addressed.

Conclusions

Our consideration of the administrative practicalities has led us to conclude that the proposals made earlier in the Report are administratively feasible, particularly when account is taken of the fact that they will be phased in over a period of time. The introduction of graduation will involve some increase in the workload of the Inland Revenue, but there will also be some simplifications of the tax system which will liberate administrative resources. The efficient organisation of the Revenue, and the provision of a proper level of staffing, will no doubt be priorities for a Labour government. Proper enforcement of taxation and the countering of avoidance and evasion raise a wide range of issues which we have reviewed above. We recommend that a Labour government should have a substantial legislative programme on issues of enforcement, in addition to the structural tax changes which have been proposed in earlier chapters.

Conclusions

Recommendations for the reform of direct taxation

The graduation of the income tax structure and the re-structuring of National Insurance contributions would involve:

Recommendation 1: The present 25 per cent/40 per cent rate structure for income tax should be replaced by a sequence of rates, which would start below the basic rate inherited from the Conservatives and rise to 50 per cent by a series of steps (page 32). The initial rate of tax in this graduated structure should cover a relatively wide band (page 103).

Recommendation 2: The structure of employee National Insurance contributions be made fully progressive by abolishing the upper earnings limit, by charging a zero rate on earnings below the threshold (page 63). In the case of the self-employed, Class 2 contributions should be abolished and the lower threshold for Class 4 aligned with that for Class 1 (page 64).

Consideration of the tax treatment of married couples, of single parents, and of the elderly led us to:

Recommendation 3: The basic principle of taxation for husbands and wives should be full independence. The single person's allowance should be significantly increased and the married couple's allowance reduced at the same time, in such a way that there would be no reduction in the amount of tax-free income received by any married couple (page 37). We recommend that the single allowance and residual married couple's allowance be given as a zero-rate band (page 33 and page 39).

Recommendation 4: The additional personal allowance for single parents would be phased out with the increase in the single allowance, in the same way as the married couple's allowance, and that in the meantime it be given as a zero-rate band (page 39).

Recommendation 5: In addition, we recommend that a substantial increase in the basic National Insurance retirement pension be the occasion for the abolition of the age allowance (page 42).

Broadening the income tax base is crucial to successful tax reform in Britain, and we recommend:

Recommendation 6: The limit of £30,000 for mortgage interest relief be maintained in money terms and not increased with inflation (page 47)

Recommendation 7: The relief for mortgage interest should not be given at higher rates, but only at a single rate (page 47).

Recommendation 8: National Insurance benefits in replacement of earnings should become taxable (page 49 and page 50), at the same time as there are improvements in these benefits.

Recommendation 9: The maximum tax-free lump sum for occupational pensions should be set at £90,000 *in all cases*, including personal pensions (page 52).

Recommendation 10: Relief for remaining life assurance policies which qualify for tax relief should be half the initial rate of tax with the graduated structure (page 53).

Recommendation 11: The tax relief for private medical insurance premiums should be repealed (page 53).

Recommendation 12: The tax treatment of life assurance companies should be reviewed, and the relief for selling expenses should be completely withdrawn (page 54).

Recommendation 13: The Business Expansion Scheme should be abolished (page 55).

Recommendation 14: Tax deductibility for 50 per cent of Class 4 National Insurance contributions for the self-employed should be abolished (page 66).

Recommendation 15: The composite rate of tax should be abolished and replaced by a withholding rate, permitting non-taxpayers to claim back the tax they have paid (page 54). This withholding rate should be set at the initial graduated rate (page 103).

Recommendation 16: Tax exemption of income and gains arising under Personal Equity Plans should be abolished (page 55).

Recommendation 17: A formula should be established for the automatic adjustment of the scales for the taxation of the benefit derived from company cars, and the scale extended to tax more heavily more expensive cars (page 58).

Recommendation 18: The favourable tax treatment of share option schemes, and of profit-sharing schemes, should be repealed (page 58).

Recommendation 19: Benefits in kind, as assessed for income tax, should be subject to National Insurance contributions (page 64).

These measures would significantly reverse the erosion of the tax base that has taken place under the Conservatives. In the absence of *effective* introduction of these measures, we would recommend:

Recommendation 20: There be a limit to the total allowances and relief that may be claimed (page 59).

In addition, we recommend:

Recommendation 21: All means-tested social security benefits should be tax-free, repealing the taxation of income support for the unemployed or those involved in trade disputes (page 49).

Recommendation 22: Provision of employer-subsidised nurseries for children should not be a chargeable benefit for income tax purposes (page 57).

The tax burden on earnings, on which much attention is focussed, may be reduced if it is shared more fully with investment income. The broadening of the tax base just described will contribute to that end, but we also recommend:

Recommendation 23: Investment income received by those aged under a specified age should be subject to a social security tax, parallel to the National Insurance contributions paid on earned incomes (page 65).

Recommendation 24: The income and capital gains of pension funds should be subject to a special tax at the same rate as the social security tax on investment income (page 52).

In the case of capital gains, we would take further the measures introduced in the 1988 Budget:

Recommendation 25: Capital gains should be aggregated with other income for the purposes of calculating the tax rate applicable, which would also include the social security tax (page 70). The annual exemption should be substantially reduced and retirement relief should be reduced by the same proportion (page 71). Death should be treated as deemed realisation and tax charged.

Capital transfer taxes have been eroded under the Conservatives. We recommend:

Recommendation 26: The reform of capital transfer taxation should be a matter of priority for the next Labour Government. The Committee has a preference for a recipient-based tax, either a lifetime capital receipts tax (page 75) or that gifts and bequests should be charged to income tax (page 77). It would however also regard a return to an effective capital transfer tax as a realistic option (page 75).

In the field of company taxation, the Committee reviewed the case for major changes in the tax base but believes that the argument for stability in corporate tax arrangements outweighs any possible advantages of alternative structures. It recommends:

Recommendation 27: A future Labour Chancellor should give consideration (a) to the rate of imputation (page 83) and (b) to Britain playing an active role in securing European harmonisation of corporate taxation (page 84).

In the case of sole traders and partnerships, to secure equity between the self-employed and employed and greater clarity in tax arrangements, we recommend:

Recommendation 28: The basis of assessment for business income should be the current year, with tax payable on account during the year in which it arises (page 78).

Recommendation 29: There should be a review by the Inland Revenue of the provisions for deductions of business expenses (page 79).

In the case of employer National Insurance contributions, we recommend:

Recommendation 30: Employer contributions should be re-structured so that a single rate is payable on all earnings above the lower earnings limit (page 67). The base should be extended to include fringe benefits (page 67).

In the case of local taxation, the Committee considered the possibilities offered by a local income tax and capital value rates to replace the poll tax. It recommends:

Recommendation 31: A serious examination should be made of a capital value rate as an eventual replacement of the poll tax, to be accompanied by a regional income tax if constitutional changes are to be made to institute regional assemblies (page 98).

The Committee wishes however to stress that the introduction of such an alternative to the poll tax will be a slow process, and recommends in the meantime:

Recommendation 32: Measures should be taken to alleviate the worst distributional features of the poll tax, and in particular that it should be 100 per cent rebated for those on low incomes (page 96).

Our consideration of the administrative practicalities has led us to conclude that the proposals made in the Report are administratively feasible, particularly when account is taken of the fact that they will be phased in over a period of time. The introduction of graduation will involve some increase in the workload of the Inland Revenue, but there will also be some simplifications of the tax system which will liberate administrative resources. We recommend:

Recommendation 33: The efficient organisation of the Revenue, and the provision of a proper level of staff should be a priority for a Labour Government (page 107). Consideration should be given to more effective methods of countering avoidance and evasion (pages 107–110).

The recommendations described above represent, in our judgement, a feasible and effective way of reforming direct taxation in Britain. The themes are:
- a fair graduation of the tax burden;
- genuine independence for wives and husbands;
- lower rates of tax on a broader base;
- a fairer sharing of the burden on earned and unearned income;
- ending the "voluntary" nature of inheritance tax;
- local taxation according to ability to pay.

We believe these themes have electoral appeal and are in accord with a clear set of principles for the future of the British tax system.

References and sources for Charts and Tables

Chapter 3

Chart 3.1 The tax burden in OECD countries: "International Comparisons of Taxes and Social Security Contributions in 20 OECD Countries 1976-1986", *Economic Trends*, January 1989.

Chart 3.2 Tax ratio 1974/5 to 1989/90: Derived from *Financial Statement and Budget Report 1989-90*, HM Treasury, Table 1.2 and equivalents from earlier years.

Chart 3.3 The tax structure in 1988/9: *Financial Statement and Budget Report 1989-90*, HM Treasury, Table 1.2.

Chart 3.4 Direct tax burdens by earnings levels: *Hansard*, 10th January 1989, col. 634w.

Chart 3.5 Direct and indirect tax burdens by earnings levels: *Hansard*, 10th January 1989, col. 634w.

Chapter 5

Table on page 29 Income tax burden: Figures for mean male earnings from *British Labour Statistics Historical Abstract 1886-1968*, Table 41, and *New Earnings Survey 1989*, Table A15.

Chart 5.1 Average tax rates and income levels: *National Income and Expenditure 1959*, CSO, Table 22, and *Economic Trends*, November 1987, Appendix 4. The income levels are adjusted to 1978/9 using an index of average taxable income constructed from the above sources for 1959 and 1984/5 and from *National Income and Expenditure 1979* for 1978/9. These are then adjusted to 1988/89 levels using 'total personal income before tax' from *Monthly Digest of Statistics* January 1984, Table 1.4, and November 1989, Table 1.5. The index is finally brought forward to 1989/90 by assuming an 8 per cent growth in incomes from 1988/9. This adjustment is necessarily approximate but is the same for both years plotted on the Chart.

Chapter 7
Table 7.1 Inland Revenue estimates of cost of tax reliefs and exemptions: *Government Expenditure Plans 1989-90 to 1991-92,* Cm621, Table 21.1.25, and *Government Expenditure Plans, 1988-89 to 1990-91,* Cm 288-I, Table 6.5.

Chart 7.1 Mortgage interest tax relief ceiling: Dwelling prices for new building society mortgages from *Housing and Construction Statistics 1976-1986,* Table 10.11, and *Housing and Construction Statistics, March 1989 part 1,* Table 1.13.

Chapter 8
Chart 8.1 Earnings distribution and employees NIC schedule: Earnings distributions from *New Earnings Survey 1989,* Table A14.

Chapter 10
Curran J and R Burrows: "National profiles of the self-employed" in *Employment Gazette,* Department of Employment, July 1989.

Chapter 11
Table 11.1 Local authority income and expenditure 1979-80 and 1989-90: *Financial, General and Rating Statistics 1979/80,* CIPFA, and *Financial and General Statistics 1989-90,* CIPFA.

Chart 11.1 Local authority current expenditure by service 1989-90: *Financial and General Statistics 1989-90,* CIPFA.

Kay J and S Smith: *Local Income Tax: Options for the introduction of a local income tax in the UK,* IFS Report Series No. 31, 1988.

Chapter 12
"International tax avoidance and evasion: four related studies", *Issues in international taxation,* no. 1, OECD, 1987.

Taxation Review Background Papers

1 *The impact of the 1988 income tax changes*, Holly Sutherland (November 1988)

2 *Restructuring National Insurance contributions*, A. B. Atkinson (December 1988)

3 *The Field/Ormerod tax reform proposals*, A. B. Atkinson & H. Sutherland (February 1989)

4 *Taxation, the Poverty Trap and the 1989 Budget*, A. B. Atkinson & H. Sutherland (April 1989)

5 *Direct and Indirect Taxation: a Socialist Approach*, Henry Neuburger (May 1989)

These are all available from the Fabian Society, 11 Dartmouth Street, London SW1H 9BN, price £3.50 each (inc p&p). Please send payment with order (cheques payable to *Fabian Society*). Or order by telephone, quoting Access, Barclaycard or Visa number.

Index